Tulsi

The Mother Medicine of Nature

Dr. Narendra Singh
&
Dr. Yamuna Hoette

with
Dr. Ralph Miller

Published by   :   International Institute of Herbal Medicine (IIHM)
                        2/301, Vijay Khand-II, Gomti Nagar,
                        Lucknow - 226 010
                        e-mail : drnsingh@avadh.net

First Edition 2002
International Edition

M.R.P. Rs. 251.00

ISBN 81-88007-00-5

_____

Typeset in Garamond 12/14.4. Layout, design and printing by
Alpana Arts, Lucknow/Delhi. (http://www.alpanaarts.com)
Cover Photo : Ashish Maurya

Dedications

This book is dedicated in the loving memory of my mother Surya Devi and my aunt Smt. Nirmal Chhabra (Nirmal means pure), fondly called "Tooni", who always inspired me to love nature and God. Tulsi was their favorite deity. I am also indebted to my wife Savitri for her unspoken life-long support for all my research work.

Narendra

This book is dedicated to my beloved Guruji, Shri H.W.L. Poonjaji, called Papaji, who is a source of truth, light, knowledge, inspiration and the ultimate healing power. He has given me Tulsi leaves to cure my ailments on many occasions.

Yamuna

Contents

About the authors

Dr. Narendra Singh

Dr. Narendra Singh was born in 1935 in Kamhenpur village in Azamgarh District of Uttar Pradesh, India, and was brought up in a traditional well-educated Rajput family. His education, from initial schooling to doctorate of medicine, was completed at Azamgarh, Allahabad, Agra and Lucknow. Dr. Singh is a follower of the ancient customs, culture and Vedic tenets of Hinduism. As a child he acquired knowledge of Sanskrit, the Hindu epic Ramayana and the old scriptures of Hinduism from his grandfathers and great-grandfather. This childhood educational influence inspired him to be a doctor or scientist so as to be able to scientifically study Ayurveda and medicinal herbs.

Dr. Singh's knowledge of allopathic medicine and pharmacology has greatly enhanced his herbal research studies. All the medicinal herbs mentioned in the ancient Hindu texts drew interest. He applied his time and energy to the task of researching their medicinal value and possible actions, and investigating the ways herbs sustained human civilization for millennia before the existence of modern drugs. He has tried to amalgamate mythology, ancient Ayurvedic practices and modern experimental and clinical research, to find the most effective use of herbs for the benefit of humanity. Tulsi formed the nucleus of his research work of more than three decades. Many of Dr. Singh's ideas have been controversial, as his research work often deviated from routine modern scientific methods, yet his findings are highly convincing. In the area of herbal medicine, Dr. Singh has more than 250 papers published in professional journals and proceedings of scientific conferences.

Dr. Singh is the former head of the Regional Ayurvedic Research Institute in Lucknow, and is currently director of the

International Institute of Herbal Medicine and president of both The International Society for Herbal Medicine and The International Society of Asian Traditional Medicine. He was the elected chairman of two conferences- (1) "Conference on Current Biotechnological Trends in Medicinal Plants Research" in 1993 held at National Research Laboratory for Conservation of Cultural Property (Govt. of India) Lucknow (INDIA) and (2) World Congress on Biotechnological Developments in Medicinal substances of Plants and "Marine Origin" in1995 at King George's Medical College, Lucknow. Besides he was Secretary: International Relations Indian Pharmacological Society, a body of International Union of Pharmacologists (IUPHAR). He has been and is still referee and on the editorial board of several International and National Scientific Journals.

Dr. Christine (Yamuna) Hoette

Dr. Christine Hoette was born in 1954 in Erlangen, Germany, and finished her undergraduate education in Coburg, Germany. She earned her Medical Doctor degree in 1984, after studies in Paris and Munich. She then practiced internal medicine in a city hospital (Department of Internal Medicine and Cardiology) in Munich. In 1992, she gave up her practice in Germany in order to come to India to serve and live with her Guru, H.W.L. Poonjaji. Until his passing, she acted as his personal physician as well as physician to the international community of devotees around him in Lucknow, India. During this time, Poonjaji introduced her to the essence of Ayurveda. Her background in allopathic medicine, combined with the years of deep initiation into the heart of Ayurvedic knowledge, qualified her to coauthor this book with Dr. Narendra Singh.

Acknowledgments

The authors are most indebted to Dr. Syed Sadiq Abbas, Ph.D. and to Dr. (Ms.) Vandana Singh, Ph.D., scientists at the International Institute of Herbal Medicine, who provided invaluable help in collecting data and preparing the text of this book.

We are also most grateful to Sri B.S. Kanwar from Himachal Pradesh, a ninety-year-old veteran Ayurvedic expert, who helped us immensely in understanding and collecting Ayurvedic Tulsi formulae. We are grateful for the timely technical advises of Captain Yashwant Chhabra (Master of the Ship). Thanks are also due to Baledin, the young lad who is of great help to Dr. Singh in his work.

Furthermore, we are grateful to Smt. Shilpi Singh, a student of Lucknow University, and Dr. Anubha Singh, Ph.D., scientist at the National Institute of Pharmaceutical Education and Research, Chandigarh, for their help in the collection of literature from various libraries in India.

We are indebted to Late Prof. K.P. Bhargava, M.D., Ph.D. (Utah, USA), Late Prof. R.P. Kohli, M.D., Prof. G.P. Gupta, M.D., Late Prof. K.K. Tangri, M.D., Prof. K.N. Dhawan, M.D. and Drs. M.L. Gupta, M.D., T.K. Gupta, M.D., J.N. Sinha, M.D., V.K. Kulshreshtha, M.D., (Mrs.) Nisha Misra, M.D., (Mrs.) Renu Nath, M.D., K.S. Dixit, M.D., S. Vrat, M.D., T.N. Bhalla, M.D., R.K. Srivastava, M.D., A.K. Saxena, M.D., C. Nath, M.D., G. Palit, M.D., Prakash Verma, M.D., Pradeep Kumar, M.D., S.P. Singh, M.D., Satpal Singh, M.D., V.S. Tomar, M.B.B.S., K. Shanker, Ph.D., Asha Lata, Ph.D., Reena Kalsi, Ph.D., Shivani Pandey, Ph.D. and other technical members of the staff of the Dept. of Pharmacology and Therapeutics, King George's Medical College, who have been involved with us for three decades researching Tulsi and other herbs. The authors acknowledge with gratitude the research work of other scientists quoted in this book. Our indebtedness will always be due to the souls of those animals who were sacrificed in our research for the cause of human health.

We thank loved ones Holly, Bharat, Santosh, Amrita, Vinod Sharma, Radha, Vikas, Rahul, Dinesh, Vivek, Dayal, Mohan and Sam for their all round help.

Special thanks are due to Dr. Ralph Miller, Ph.D., of Canada, for his invaluable editorial input and for drafting various sections of this monograph.

Editors : Dr. Vandana Singh & Dr. Syed Sadiq Abbas

Preface

Around the world, people are becoming increasingly interested in herbs for their nutritional and medicinal properties. This awareness and interest has grown during the past three decades in response to the increase in environmental pollution, the deterioration of food quality, the fast, competitive and unhealthy modern lifestyle, the increase in various degenerative diseases, and the adverse side effects of many modern allopathic drugs and other high technology medical interventions. We live in a disturbed biosphere; both our outer and inner environments are out of balance – life itself on planet Earth is threatened.

Tulsi, the sacred basil (*Ocimum sanctum*), is one of the holiest plants of modern Indians, as well as the Aryans ancient inhabitants of India. Renowned for its health-promoting and disease-preventing properties, Tulsi has captivated the human imagination since before the time of the *Rigveda* (book of eternal knowledge) written around 5000 BC.

The material in this book has been presented for the Indian reader who is familiar with Indian mythology and Ayurveda, as well as for the Western reader who may possess little or no knowledge of these matters. We are aware that the background in mythology and Ayurveda of the Indian and Western reader is very different and we have attempted to compensate accordingly. The Indian reader might find certain paragraphs too simplistic or detailed in explanation, but the text is more intelligible for the Western reader in this expanded version.

A sampling of the mythological knowledge about Tulsi is offered in Chapter I, which also describes how Tulsi has been useful as a medicinal herb and protector of life for millennia.

Chapter II describes the botanical identity, chemical characteristics and varieties of Tulsi.

People from other parts of the world, and even in India where Ayurveda has been practiced for thousands of years, do not know the exact tenets of Ayurveda. Many only know that Ayurveda is a form of natural treatment where many herbs are used, and that Ayurvedic medicines are relatively harmless in comparison to many allopathic drugs. Chapter III gives a brief and simple introduction to the science of Ayurveda for the layperson.

Chapter IV deals with "stress", not in the

common sense of the English word, but in the medical sense, as a causative factor for disease. This will enable the reader to better understand the need for an agent like Tulsi, which prevents and treats the ill effects of the numerous stressors present in modern life. Unfortunately, stress-treating agents are not well described in modern medical textbooks and are generally not taught in standard medical studies and paramedical curricula. This book provides an introduction to the prevention and treatment of stress-related diseases through antistress plants such as Tulsi.

Chapter V is a simplified summary of the scientific work on Tulsi that has been carried out in our laboratories over the last three decades. For the lay reader, and the scientist as well, our research has been presented in a manner that gives an insight into the mechanism of stress-related diseases and the pharmacological actions of Tulsi through animal experiments and human clinical trials. These studies provide convincing evidence of many of the beneficial properties of Tulsi that have been noted in the ancient mythological texts and *materia medica* of India.

Chapter VI conveys related research carried out by scientists from India and abroad. This work further confirms our contention that Tulsi is a potent adaptogen/ antistress agent.

Chapter VII provides summary explanations and conclusions drawn from our studies and research review, integrated with inferences from mythological sources and Ayurvedic literature. In the end, we emphasize, after much simplification of the scientific facts about Ayurveda and stress-disease phenomena, that the herb Tulsi is ideal for promotion of health and prevention of and treatment of disease as a general tonic and antistress/adaptogenic agent.

Appendix A describes some typical clinical cases demonstrating Tulsi's therapeutic effects. Appendix B provides recommendations for the use of Tulsi tea (chai) or capsules in a variety of stress-related diseases. Appendix C focuses on some of the special benefits of Tulsi for the elderly.

Footnotes are marked F1, F2, F3 etc. and are found on the bottom of the pages. To facilitate understanding, a glossary of medical terms is provided after the main text. References are identified in the text by the author's name(s) and date of publication, and are listed alphabetically in the bibliography and indices are given at the end of the book. The inside of back-page gives article on usefulness of *Ocimum sanctum* (Globe Magazine USA, 1986), which is a representation of our continued research on Tulsi.

Modern research, combined with centuries of intimate worship and study of Tulsi in conditions of health and disease, calls for the knowledge of this agent, one of nature's finest healing herbs, to be spread globally for the benefit of humanity. With this aim, the authors have tried their best to present a thorough and accurate summary of the health benefits of Tulsi. Of course, scientific knowledge is in a continuous state of evolution and differences of opinion exist in matters of research interpretation and conclusions. Readers are encouraged to confirm the information presented herein with other scientific resources and their own experience.

Introduction

Ralph D. Miller, Ph.D.

Tulsi Queen of Herbs

It is a privilege to have the opportunity to write the introduction to this historic document, which presents the first extensive overview of India's legendary holy basil *Tulsi*, integrating the ancient wisdom of Ayurveda with modern experimental and clinical research. Dr. Singh and Dr. Hoette ambitiously address the major health crises of our times and provide impressive evidence for an ancient remedy.

When I was first introduced to the sacred Tulsi[F1] some years back, my first reaction, as a Western scientist, was disbelief. This can't be so, I thought. This herb sounds too good to be true. There seemed to be far more wide-ranging health benefits attributed to this plant than could be possible for a single agent. Yet, I realized that there must be a compelling reason why Tulsi has, for thousands of years, remained one of the most cherished of India's sacred healing plants. Furthermore, in addition to being a pillar of the traditional Ayurvedic holistic health system, Tulsi continues to be spiritually honored daily by millions. So, it really can't be much of a

surprise to discover that modern science is accumulating evidence in support of many of the traditional health promotion and disease treatment uses of Tulsi.

Much of this experimental and clinical research documentation has been provided by Dr. Narendra Singh and his colleagues, and is summarized in this book alongwith relevant findings of other scientists. Narendraji has been a pioneer in the modern investigation of traditional Ayurvedic medicines for over three decades, being perhaps best known for his research on the antistress/adaptogenic properties of Indian plants – especially Tulsi and Ashwagandha.

The research reviewed in the following chapters offers impressive evidence that Tulsi protects against and reduces stress, enhances stamina and endurance, increases the body's efficient use of oxygen, boosts the immune system, slows aging, and provides a rich supply of antioxidants and other nutrients. These general vitality-enhancing properties, which support and enhance the body's natural capacity to maintain a state of well-being, likely account for much of the impressively wide range of Tulsi's traditional health promoting uses. Amongst its array of more

---

[F1] Tulsi is pronounced "tool-see" in English.

specific effects, the data indicate that Tulsi reduces inflammation, prevents gastric ulcers, protects against radiation, lowers fevers, cholesterol and high blood pressure, enhances periodontal health, displays significant natural antibacterial, antiviral and antifungal activity, improves digestion and absorption of other nutrients, and even repels mosquitoes and other potentially harmful insects. It would appear that Tulsi offers remarkable preventative and curative potential with respect to many degenerative disorders, such as cancer, heart disease, arthritis, diabetes and neurological dementia.

In the following section I have attempted to provide a social and medical context within which Tulsi, and other treasures of traditional Indian medicine, will undoubtedly soon emerge in modern health care practices worldwide.

Cultural perspectives on health and well-being

Various approaches to achieving and maintaining optimal health and well-being have developed in different societies throughout human history. Long-standing, traditional cultures around the world have tended to emphasize holistic concepts, such as equilibrium, balance and harmony with oneself, nature and the spiritual realm. Integrated health systems evolved over thousands of years in which specific problems and disorders were considered within a broad biological, social lifestyle and spiritual context, encompassing general health promotion as well as the treatment of specific disorders of mind and body. The ancient Eastern systems of Indian Ayurveda and traditional Chinese medicine are perhaps the best known and documented examples of these broad holistic health approaches. In contrast, modern

Western medicine evolved from its early Greek roots to emphasize the relative isolation and out-of-context analysis of separate physical components and disorders of the body, with primary focus on the treatment of specific aspects of disease.

The health systems of the ancient cultures are generally grounded in a sophisticated knowledge of local environmental conditions, nutrients and herbal medicines. The industrialized West has, until very recently, tended to discard traditional nature-based, dietary and lifestyle approaches in favor of reliance on isolated compounds or synthetic drugs, and sophisticated surgical and other "high tech" diagnostic and remedial procedures. These varying cultural health perspectives can be seen as emphasizing different points on a continuum, encompassing the holistic promotion of general health and well-being on one end, through the prevention of anticipated high-risk disorders, to the specific therapeutic treatment of ongoing diseases and disabilities at the other end of the health care dimension.

Modern Western medical science has made major advances in the understanding of basic anatomy and physiology, the role of germs and hygiene in disease, and the identification and diagnosis of physical disorder. Effective methods have been developed for handling emergency physical crises, preventing many infectious conditions and curing a wide variety of communicable diseases. However, the Western medical system has not been able to cope with the growing array of chronic degenerative environmental, lifestyle and stress-related physical and mental disorders that plague modern society. These latter conditions are the leading factors in illness and premature death in the West - and are currently vastly overloading and bankrupting the public medical systems throughout the industrialized nations of the world. Furthermore, the same stress-related diseases are now emerging as health crises in developing nations worldwide.

In addition to major personal dietary, exercise and other lifestyle factors, the mental and biological stresses caused by the demanding and rapidly changing physical and social environments of modern urban life have introduced a non-specific malaise of epidemic proportions, which the traditionally fragmented approach of modern medicine is ill equipped to handle. These are some of the central topics addressed in this book, which makes a strong case for a major role for holistic Ayurvedic perspectives, and Tulsi in particular, in the prevention and treatment of these pervasive modern illnesses.

While the contrast in emphasis between the traditional Oriental integrated way-of-life health systems and the narrower, more specific disease treatment orientation of modern Western medicine remains prominent, broad concepts of general health promotion have received increasing international attention in recent decades. The World Health Organization (WHO) signified this broadening shift in perspective in 1946 with its definition: "Health is a state of complete physical, mental and social well-being, and not merely the absence of disease or infirmity." The importance of inner peace and spiritual harmony has been emphasized, as well. In 1978, WHO recommended that traditional health and folk medicine approaches be integrated with modern medical therapies, stressing the necessity of ensuring rapport and collaboration among practitioners of the various systems. This Tulsi book, and the research it documents, represents a significant step in this direction.

The West is clearly in the midst of a major paradigm shift away from its former almost exclusively reactive disease-oriented therapeutic and preventative system, managed by medical personnel, to a more pro-active, multidisciplinary, public health promotion approach. In addition to a rapidly expanding reliance on "alternative" or "complementary" health care practitioners, a significant "self-care revolution" is clearly underway, in which individuals are increasingly taking charge of their own health. There is growing public and professional awareness that many non-medical aspects of day-to-day life can significantly favor health or be harmful to it. In addition to biological fitness, general quality of life issues, including spiritual, dietary, lifestyle, political/economic and environmental factors, are now recognized as essential components of a positive, healthy society.

This positive evolution in modern health perspectives includes the growing scientific examination and verification of many previously unexplored or prematurely rejected traditional treatments and holistic systems for achieving and maintaining optimal health. The investigation of Tulsi's health promoting properties is one of the rapidly expanding research areas sure to bear rich fruit. Currently little known in the West, Tulsi is certain to emerge in the near future as a major player in the growing field of herbal supplements and medicines, both in daily self-care and in professionally-managed health care systems.

Ralph D. Miller, *Ph.D., is vice president of the International Society for Herbal Medicine and founder of The Green Isle Enterprise, which is devoted to holistic health, psychology and education. Dr. Miller is a former Director of Research for the Canadian National Department of Health and Welfare, and is the author of* <u>Cannabis and Its Effects</u>, <u>Drugs and Their Effects</u> *and numerous other publications.*

History and Mythology of Tulsi

Introducing Tulsi

In India, the herb Tulsi[F2] (sometimes spelled "Tulasi") has been widely known for its health promoting and medicinal value for thousands of years. Commonly called sacred or holy basil, it is a principal herb of Ayurveda, the ancient traditional holistic health system of India. Tulsi is known as "The Incomparable One", "The Mother Medicine of Nature", and "The Queen of Herbs".

Ayurveda, in *Sanskrit* [F3], means "knowledge of life". Herbs lie at the very heart of Ayurvedic practice. Ayurvedic knowledge was born from the wisdom of the ancient *rishis* (sages and healers) and *yogis* (ascetics practicing yoga) of India, and was first passed on from healer to healer as an oral tradition for untold generations before the earliest

known texts were written around 5000 BC. The *Rigveda* is the first documented scientific record of Ayurveda (Griffith, 1963). *Rig* means "in verses" and *veda* [F4] means "book of infinite knowledge". The *Rigveda* emphasizes the great importance of herbs for optimal health and well-being. The main verse (*sloka*) of this book states:

ओं द्यौः शान्तिरन्तरिक्ष शान्तिः पृथिवी शान्तिरायः
शान्ति–औषधयः शान्तिः
वनस्पतयः शान्तिर्विश्वेदेवाः शान्तिर्ब्रह्म शान्तिः
सर्व शान्तिः शान्तिरेव शान्तिः सा मा शान्तिरेधि।
(ऋग्वेद)

"The sun should be a giver of happiness, the sky should be a giver of happiness, all trees and plants should be givers of happiness. All

---

[F2] In *Sanskrit* Tulsi is known by many names, including *Surasah, Ajaka, Parnasa, Manjari, Haripriya* (the beloved of Lord Vishnu) and *Bhutagni* (the dstroyer of demon). Hindu denominations defer in how they regard the Tulsi plants as the Goddess. Generally worshipers of Lord Vishnu revere Tulsi as *Lakshmi* or *Vrinda*, devotees of Lord Rama honor Tulsi as *Sita*, while followers of Lord Krishna vernerate Tulsi as *Vrinda, Radha* and *Rukmani*. There are many other different names of Tulsi in the various languages and dialect of India.

[F3] *Sanskrit* is considered the oldest recorded language.

[F4] The *Vedas* are the most ancient scriptures of the Hindus.

these should give us peace of mind (*shanti*) and even the peace should give us peace".

The Ayurvedic approach is highly respectful towards all creation and sees the whole universe as one divine unity. Hinduism is generally viewed in the West as the main religion of India. However, it is not a religion in the ordinary sense; it is rather known as *dharma*, which in Sanskrit means "way of life". Hinduism is a way of being which respects the delicate balance between all forces of nature, especially the coexistence of humans and nature, and Ayurveda is the practical expression of this dharma. Ayurveda has evolved since its early beginnings into one of the most comprehensive and respected holistic approaches to health and well-being.

The knowledge of Ayurveda, first written down in the ancient Vedas, was further described 2000 years later (2700 to 600 BC) in the Ayurvedic *samhitas* (textbooks). Especially important are those by Carak (*Carak Samhita*, 1949) and Susrut (*Susrut Samhita*, 1938) who documented the medical knowledge of their time with the help of their disciples. The *Carak Samhita* is primarily a book on medical therapeutics, describing herbal health tonics and rejuvenators for longevity and prevention of disease, as well as daily regimens for better living, including diet which varies for different body types and different diseases. The text integrates the art and science

of living. It is impressive to see how much knowledge currently taught in modern sciences, such as botany, pharmacology, anatomy and physiology (including the circulation of blood and lymph), is described in detail in the *Carak Samhita*.

In reading these ancient scriptures, we become aware of the utmost importance of herbal medicine for maintaining well-being, preventing disease, restoring health and prolonging life. In such scriptures as *Vagbhata* [F5] (Godbole *et al.,* 1966), *Nighantu Adarsha* (Vaidya, 1985), *Agnipurana* [F6] (Vedavyasa, 1966), *Vishnupurana* (Garg, 1982), *Padmapurana* (Vedvyasa, 1960), *Garudapurana* (Vedavyasa, 1964; Shastri, 1968) and *Tulsi Kavacham* (Dymock *et al.,* 1893), written between 500 BC and 1200 AD, the plant Tulsi is continuously mentioned as one of the main pillars of herbal medicine. Early references describing Ayurvedic, Unani [F7] and folklore uses of Tulsi are noted by Dymock *et al.,* (1893); Nadkarni, (1908-revised, 1982); Kirtikar and Basu, (1935); Varier, (1996); Sharma, (1999) and Chopra *et al.,* (1996).

Tulsi use in daily life and worship

In the ancient scriptures, Tulsi holds the supreme place among the various medicinal herbs. The *Padmapurana* and the *Tulsi Kavacham* describe Tulsi as a protector of life, accompanying the human being from birth

---

[F5] *Vagbhata* (Godbole *et al.,* 1966) (800 AD) and *Nighantus* (Vaidya, 1985) (800 AD) are later Ayurvedic textbooks elaborating on this knowledge. *Bhagwan* (Lord) Dhanvantri, called the 'Founder of Ayurveda' wrote the original *Nighantu*, which was revised by rishi Kashyapa in 800 AD. The saying goes that Dhanvantri was born with an "*amrit kumbha*" (jar of nectar) in his hands, after the *Devas* (Gods) and *Rakshasas* (Demons) had churned the ocean.

[F6] *Purana* means ancient historical scripture, adjective: *pauranic.*

[F7] Unani, meaning Greek in Arabic, is a system of healthcare that incorporate Greek, Arabic and Ayurvedic medicine. Unani is thought to have originated with the teachings of the Greek philosopher and physician Hipporactes (460-377 BC). Around 10th century AD, it was introduced to India, with the spread of Islamic civilization, where it was combined with prior Indian systems of medicine including Ayurveda. Today, India is one of the leading countries in Unani medical practice and research.

up till death (Dymock *et al*, 1893). The *Pauranic* mythology calls Tulsi *Vishnu Priya*, "Beloved of Lord Vishnu"[F8]. In the *Bhagavata* and *Mahabharata* (ancient holy epics and scriptures), it is described how Tulsi, a goddess and devotee of Lord Vishnu, was ultimately re-incarnated as the plant Tulsi. It is said that in order to express her devotion to her beloved Lord, she took this form as a herb which would be offered in worship and service to Him (Garg, 1982).

The ancient rishis insured the integration of Tulsi into daily life by incorporating it in religious rituals. Hindus perform *pujas* (religious rituals) several times a month on auspicious occasions. The rishis included leaves of the primary three varieties of Tulsi (Rama, Krishna and Vana Tulsi) in the *Charanamrita* [F9] of the puja. In this way people at all levels of society routinely consumed Tulsi to their health benefit during worship in their temples and households. As a sacred plant and goddess, Tulsi is worshipped and venerated daily by traditional Hindus, and is part of all such households today. It is typically grown in an earthen pot in the family home or garden.

A mythological example from the scriptures

Various passages of the *Padmapurana* reveal the importance of Tulsi in Indian mythology. Lord Shiva described the power of Tulsi to the rishi Narada (the omnipresent and eternal rishi and devotee of Lord Vishnu), saying:

"Oh, Narada! Every house, every village, every forest, wherever the plant of Tulsi is grown, there misery, fear, disease and poverty do not exist. Tulsi in all aspects and places is holier than holy. Where the breeze blows through Tulsi plants, it spreads Tulsi's fragrance making the surrounding area pious and pure. Lord Vishnu and other gods shower their blessings on the people who worship and grow Tulsi. Through the worship of Tulsi, the souls of all our ancestors are pleased and our path to the heavens is opened. Oh Narada! The three gods, Brahma, Vishnu and Rudra[F10] reside in the roots, middle parts of the plant and in the flowering tops respectively. This is why the plant of Tulsi is the most holy plant of the earth. Those who plant and nurture Tulsi in the Shiva temple or in any other place of worship, such as Naimisharayand[F11] and Prayag [F12], are twice blessed by the gods. The offering of Tulsi leaves to Lord Vishnu/Krishna should be considered the best way of worshipping Him."

After this, rishi Narada requested Lord Shiva to tell him about the *Triratri Vrata* (three nights fast) *Tulsi Vrata* (Tulsi fast). Lord Shiva described then the details of this vrata to rishi Narada in several holy mantras. He said:

"Oh, Narada! You have to keep awake for three nights, worshipping Vishnu and Laxmi with flowers, fruits, Ganga water and Tulsi leaves. This vrata helps one to learn the art and science of music and dance if those are practiced during this period of fast."

[F8] Vishnu is one of the three supreme gods of Hindus. Brahma represents the Creator, Vishnu the Preserver and Shiva the Destroyer.

[F9] Literally, "Nectar from the feet of God". When the devotee forgets his ego and touches the feet of God, he receives the blessings in the form of the *Charanamrita*. It traditionally consists of cow's milk, yogurt, honey, Ganga water and Tulsi leaves, and is offered by the worshipper to the deity, blessed during the ritual and, returned afterwards by the Hindu priest. This *prasad* (offering) is later consumed by the devotee.

[F10] Rudra is the destructive aspect of Lord Shiva.

[F11] Naimisharayana is a holy place near Lucknow, Uttar Pradesh, where many revered rishis resided, such as Vedavyash, the writer of the *Mahabharata*, which contains the *Bhagvad Geeta*.

[F12] Prayag is the confluence of the rivers Ganga, Yamuna and the mythical Saraswati.

The *Padmapurana* states:

पत्रं पुष्पं फलं मूलं शाखा त्वक् स्कन्धसंशितम्।
तुलसीसंभवं सर्व पावनं मृत्तिकादिकम्।।
(*पद्मपुराण* 24/2)

Leaves, flowers, fruits, root, branches and the main stem and everything about Tulsi is sacred; even the soil under the Tulsi plant is holy. (Padmapurana 24/2)

यद्येकं तुलसीकाष्ठं मध्ये काष्ठस्य तस्य हि ।
दाहकाले भरेन्मुक्तिः कोटिपापयुतस्य च ।।
(*पद्मपुराण* 24/2)

Even one plant of Tulsi put into the fire of the funeral pyre is capable of providing salvation (moksha) to an individual. (Padmapurana 24/2)

Botanical and Chemical Characteristics

Botanical identification

Botanists have given Tulsi (holy sacred basil), the Latin name *Ocimum sanctum*. *Ocimum* means "fragrant lipped"; *sanctum,* "sacred"; and basil derives from *basilicum,* "royal". This species includes both the green leafed *Sri* or *Rama* Tulsi and the dark green-to-purple-leafed *Shyama* or *Krishna* varieties. More recently, *Ocimum sanctum* has also become known by the name *Ocimum tenuiflorum,* meaning "basil with small flowers". A third type, *Vana* Tulsi (or forest Tulsi) is identified as *Ocimum gratissimum* "very grateful basil". *Ocimum* belongs to the mint family *Labiatae/Lamiaceae*. The shrubby Tulsi plant may grow to a height of a meter or more and the leaves may smell of peppermint, cloves, licorice or lemon, as well as having a distinct aroma of their own. A detailed description is provided in Table 1 (Srivastava, 1988; Sivarajan and Balachandran, 1994).

Rama and Krishna Tulsi are commonly cultivated in the Indian plains, as well as private homes and gardens around the country, and typically need special attention and warmth for optimal growth. Vana Tulsi is found in the Himalayas as well as the plains of India, where it readily grows untended on vacant land. Vana Tulsi is also considered sacred and can be used for health in the same way as Rama and Krishna Tulsi. Vana Tulsi is cultivated and grows wild in other parts of Asia and in Africa as well, where it is also widely used as a medicinal plant (Pushpangadan and Sobti, 1977). Hooker accurately described different varieties of Tulsi in 1872 in *Flora of British India*.

Chemical and nutritional constituents

Tulsi varies in size and potency depending on climate, nourishment and soil conditions. Chemically, Tulsi contains alkaloids, fats, carbohydrates, proteins, glycosides, phenols, saponins, tannins and terpenes. The essential oil components of Tulsi are mainly volatile terpenes and phenols. Amongst the essential oils are eugenol (a major pharmacological component), methyl eugenol, methyl ether, caryophyllene, terpinene-4-ol, decylaldehyde, salinene, alpha-pinene, beta-pinene, camphene, carvacrol, terpene-urosolic acid, ursolic acid, juvocimene I and II, thymol, rhymol, camphor, xanthomicrol, caffeate, myrcenol and nerol (Dutt, 1939; Khurana and Vagikar, 1950; Nadkarni and Patwardhan, 1952; Nigam *et al.,* 1970; Laurence *et al.,* 1972; Jain and Jain, 1973; Lal *et al.,* 1978; Maheshwari *et al.,* 1987; Gupta, 1987; Rastogi and Mehrotra, 1995a; Rastogi and Mehrotra, 1995b). Although many people find Tulsi to be uplifting and energy enhancing, it contains no caffeine or other stimulants.

Tulsi possesses a high value as a nutritional supplement, providing vitamin A (carotene, 2.5mg/100gm of fresh Tulsi leaves), vitamin C (ascorbic acid, 85mg/100gm) and minerals (for example, calcium, 0.5 to 3.5mg/100gm) in an organic, easily digestible form (Singh *et al.,* 1969; Pushpangadan and Sobti, 1977; Ornish, 1996). An analysis of a sample of our Tulsi at the Indian Institute of Technology, Kanpur also revealed the presence of iron and zinc. Manganese and sodium were found in leaves as trace elements (Samudaralwar and Garg, 1996).

Ingesting one gram of dried Tulsi leaves daily would provide about 8.5mg of natural vitamin C. This is superior to synthetic vitamin C, as the absorption is much higher - the "bioavailability" of the natural vitamin C is much greater than that of the synthetic form. The daily requirement of vitamin C is approximately 60mg (RDA – Recommended Daily Allowance in US, 1997), although much higher doses are needed for optimal health and many therapeutic effects. And, of course, various forms of basil are commonly used to improve the flavor and nutrition in many Western food recipes (Duke and Duke, 1978).

Table 1. Tulsi (*Ocimum sanctum*) botanical description and classification

Botanical description

Habit: Herb or undershrub.

Average height of the plant: 85 cm.

Root: Branched taproot.

Stem: Herbaceous, aerial, erect, quadrangular, branched, solid, pubescent, green to reddish.

Typical size of leaves: 4.3 cm long, 2.3 cm wide.

Leaf: Ramal and Cauline, opposite decussate, exstipulate, simple, petiolate, ovate, serrate, acute, pubescent, aromatic smell present, unicostate reticulate.

Inflorescence: Verticillaster.

Flower: Bracteate, pedicellate, complete, zygomorphic, hermaphrodite, pentamerous, hypogynous and cyclic.

Calyx: Sepals 5, gamosepalous, bilabiate 1/4, imbricate, persistent.

Corolla: Petals 5, gamopetalous, corolla 4/1 bilipped, imbricate.

Androecium: Stamens 4, polyandrous, epipetalous, didynamous, dithecous, dorsifixed, introrse.

Gynoecium: Bicarpellary, syncarpous, ovary superior, placentation axile, tetralocular with one ovule in each locule, a disc is present below the ovary, style gynobasic and stigma bifid.

Fruit: Carcerulus.

Floral formula: Br, %, ☿, $K_{(1/4)}$, $C_{(4/1)}$, A_{2+2}, and $G_{(2)}$.

Classification

Class: *Dicotyledoneae*

Sub-Class: *Gamopetalae*

Series: *Bicarpellatae*

Order: *Lamiales*

Family: *Labiatae/Lamiaceae*

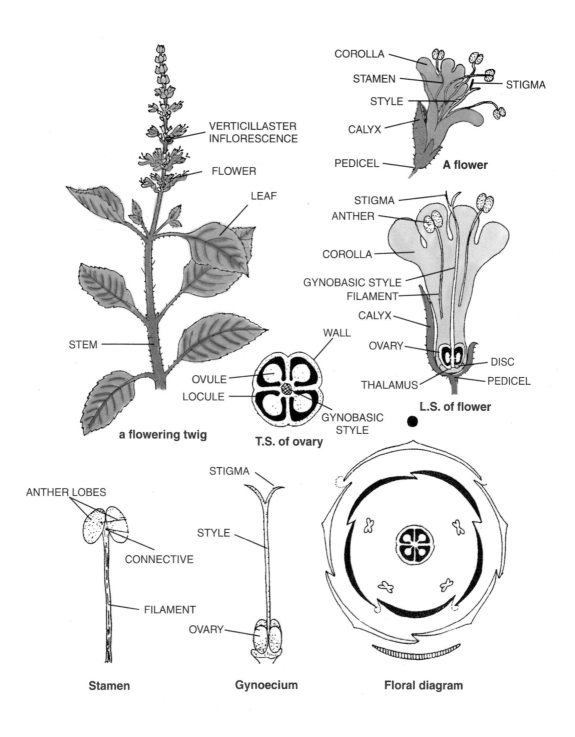

Fig 1: Tulsi (Ocimum sanctum)

3

Ayurveda: The Medicine of the Future

The efficacy and safety of Tulsi and other herbs

Insuring potency

Optimal cultivation, harvesting, preservation and storage methods are necessary for maximizing the medicinal value of plants. The efficacy and potency of Ayurvedic herbs depends upon the soil, climate, and season of collection, as the quantity of biologically active components and other chemical constituents vary according to these factors (Maheshwari *et al.,* 1987; Gupta, 1987). The ancient texts describe these issues in detail and recommend growing many medicinal herbs in the Himalayas. Nowadays, however, great quantities of herbal medicines are required for large populations and it has become necessary to cultivate these herbs in a variety of locations. Ideally, Ayurvedic farms are developed in rural areas free from environmental pollution, employing organic methods, without the use of artificial herbicides, pesticides or synthetic chemical fertilizers. Over the past 5 years, we have been able to organically cultivate Tulsi under quite ideal environmental conditions. Some scenes of our Tulsi fields are presented in Figures 2-8. Tulsi fields grown in this way spread an aroma that brings a sense of well-being and peace to the mind. Figure 7 shows Dr. Singh having such an experience in one of his Tulsi fields.

The techniques used for drying herbs are very important; too much sunlight or heat may result in loss of essential oils and other important substances of medicinal value. Herbs must be preserved and stored very carefully to maximize their potency. While some classic Ayurvedic texts describe preservation techniques, these are not always applicable in the modern era. In our times of polluted environment and bulk production of medicinal herbs, where machines are often used, specialized methods of preserving the herbs must be employed. Plants stored in damp and dusty storehouses become infected with fungi and bacteria and lose their medicinal and nutritional value and may become harmful. For optimal preservation

Fig 2 : Panoramic view of Rama Tulsi

Fig 3 : Panoramic view of Krishna Tulsi

Fig 4 : Panoramic view of Vana Tulsi

Fig 5 : The beauty of flowering Vana Tulsi

Fig 6 : Women collecting Krishna Tulsi seeds in Azamgarh

Fig 7 : Dr. N. Singh enjoying a Tulsi field

Fig 8 : An international group inspecting Tulsi fields (right to left) : Santosh Thomas Hoehne from Germany, Ofer Ishai from Israel and Vinod Sharma from India.

and storage of herbs, the location must meet several requirements: it must be clean, dry, moderate in temperature (25 to 30 degrees Celsius), well ventilated and free of direct sunshine.

Standardization and safety issues

The *safety margin* of a drug or herb is a measure of the difference between the amount of the drug necessary to produce a desired effect and the dose that would likely result in dangerous side effects – the greater the difference, the safer the drug. In experimental pharmacology, a process called *biological standardization* is often used, employing the use of animal subjects. This requires the determination of the Effective Dose 50 (ED_{50}) the dose that induces a 50% response of the desired effect, and the Lethal Dose 50 (LD_{50}) the dose that kills 50% of the animals. The *safety margin* is expressed as the ratio between the LD_{50} and the ED_{50} the larger the ratio, the safer the drug. The ED_{50} also provides a basis for an initial, preliminary estimate of the likely appropriate dose for human use. Drug dosage figures are adjusted for the weight of the subject and expressed on a drug quantity per kg body weight basis (e.g., 0.5mg/kg). After adjusting for body weight, for some drugs the approximate dose for humans is about one-twentieth of the effective dose in rats and mice, and one-fourth that in dogs. In practice, of course, this varies for different effects and different drugs.

Safety margin tests are done routinely in the pharmaceutical industry for modern, synthetic medicines. In some instances, we advise that they be carried out for herbal medicines as well, in spite of the well-known innocuous nature of the herbs in the majority of cases. For example, we have performed these tests with Tulsi, Siberian ginseng (*Eleutherococcus senticosus*), and Chinese ginseng (*Panax ginseng*), finding a very wide margin of safety for the herbs not to be found in any synthetic drugs. For Tulsi the safety margin is 306; for Siberian ginseng, 242; and for Chinese ginseng, 208. (Singh *et al.,* 1991b)

To determine the presence and quantity of the constituents of a herb, *phytochemical* [F13] analyses are employed. Such chemical analyses may reveal the quantity of specific components thought to be responsible for the medicinal activity of the herb. This is called *chemical standardization*. For example, the amount of eugenol or ursolic acid per gram of Tulsi leaves may reflect an aspect of the potency of a given lot of Tulsi. This information may provide a basis for standardizing dosages or comparing the potency of different samples. (Mediratta *et al.,* 1987)

Administration forms of Ayurvedic herbs

Generally, the best way to use Tulsi as a herbal medicine is in its raw form. If fresh whole herbs are not available, we recommend the use of herbs that are dried in the shade, or for short periods in the sun, then mildly crushed or powdered, and properly stored to preserve freshness and potency. In modern human research and clinical application, Tulsi is most commonly taken in capsule form, prepared from dried leaves. Socially, it is often prepared as *"prasadam"* and a hot water infusion or herbal tea drink.

We generally recommend the use of whole herbs so as to obtain the full synergistic interactive effects of the many bioactive constituents of the plant. Chemical extraction processes are necessarily selective, changing

[F13] Phyto: concerning a plant

the balance of the herb's constituents and their activities may alter the active components. Extracted components are usually more readily toxic as isolated chemical substances than when in natural biological context. Siberian ginseng (*Eleutherococcus senticosus*) and Chinese ginseng (*Panax ginseng*) represent good examples of this phenomenon. Although several active components (glycosides and alkaloids) have been isolated from both these plants long ago, it is the crude root that is most widely used as a health tonic around the world. The toxicity of isolated components of ginseng restricts their general use.

In addition, problems may be introduced by the toxicity of the extraction solvents themselves, in addition to their ability to sometimes modify the natural components. Deleterious changes may also occur in herbs that are ground under heat, too finely powdered, poorly stored, or boiled for too long a time during processing.

In recent years, more efficient means of whole herb extraction have been developed, such as supercritical CO_2 techniques, which offer a more complete range of the herb's constituents without solvent residues. The pharmacological properties of such extracts of Tulsi remain to be thoroughly explored.

It is difficult to obtain an injectable solution of herbs that does not create toxic side effects resulting from factors unrelated to the pharmacological activity of the constituents of interest.[F14] Such adverse reactions artifacts often complicate the interpretation of animal studies based on the injection of herbal extracts.

Dosage and treatment schedule of Ayurvedic herbs

The effects of herbal medicine generally do not depend on as rigid and predictable a dosage schedule as is typically prescribed for synthetic drugs. While biological and chemical standardization of herbs can give an idea of appropriate therapeutic dosages, the final dosage has to be adjusted individually. We have derived our recommended dosage schedule for Tulsi from traditional Ayurvedic use, animal experiments and modern clinical research. *Tulsi is generally effective in a single dose of 300 to 600mg of dried leaves daily for preventive therapy, and in 600mg to 1800mg in divided doses daily for curative therapy.* Tulsi can also be effectively taken as a pleasant herbal tea.

In comparison with many modern synthetic medicines, herbal medicines are typically given for *prolonged periods of time to prevent and treat diseases.* With clear exceptions, Ayurvedic medicine may not be effective for very acute treatment, as beneficial effects are often gradual and subtle. Increasing the acute dosage of an Ayurvedic herb beyond a certain point does not necessarily provide better efficacy; often it is the duration of treatment that is important.[F15]

[F14] For example, we found out through animal experiences that the intravenous and intraperitoneal administration of plant extracts, especially the extracts with irritant substances and essential oils, can cause thrombosis or peritonitis. Thrombosis can disturb the coronary and cerebral blood circulation and peritonitis will cause fever, even if the plant is antithrombotic and antipyretic (fever reducing).

[F15] When we began to do animal studies, we started with large doses of Tulsi, and discovered later that a treatment with small doses often has the same effect. For example, we pretreated a large number of animals with 200 to 400mg Tulsi per kg of body weight, orally in one dosage (one hour before the experiment). Later, we pretreated with a single daily dose of 20mg Tulsi per kg orally, but administered for three to six days, and got the same antistress activity on the day of the experiment.

Typical modern experimental methods of investigation cannot readily evaluate the full effect of herbs. These research tools are often more appropriate for the study of specific short-term effects of single chemical substances. Techniques of investigation must be specialized for the proper assessment of the full pharmacological activity of herbal medicines (Singh, 1986b; Singh and Misra, 1993). Herbs may have hundreds of biologically active components and observations generally have to be made over a long period. Herbs are often slow acting and may have a prolonged beneficial effect even after their administration has been discontinued. For example, after three decades of clinical research, our findings suggest that the adaptogenic/antistress activity of Tulsi, including an increase in stamina and immunological resistance, is likely to take one week to one month to develop and gives appreciable improvements in health lasting for a month or more after discontinuation.

It is obviously difficult to evaluate the medicinal properties of plant materials. Therefore, we encourage a global involvement of scientists to develop and apply new scientific methods for evaluating the ancient medicinal values of Ayurvedic herbs.

Balancing effect of natural components in herbs

Many people have moved from their natural rural habitat to big cities, where green plants are largely absent. Large populations have lost their links with their ancestral heritage and live in a synthetic, highly technological world. Likewise, modern medicine has evolved from the use of herbs to isolated and synthetic drugs. The side effects of many current synthetic drugs have caused disease conditions which were unknown to our ancestors. Gastric and duodenal ulcers caused by analgesic and anti-inflammatory agents (such as aspirin), depression by corticosteroids, and aplastic anemia by chloramphenicol are just a few examples of toxic action of common modern drugs. In contrast, Ayurvedic herbs often contain side effect balancing components that interact in a harmonious manner within the human organism, producing a generally beneficial effect. (Fig 9)

An interesting example is provided by the late Dr. I.I. Brekhman, director of the Biological Institute of Adaptation Energy of Vladivostok, USSR, who conducted a study on rats, comparing refined sugar (sucrose) to *gur* (jaggery). Gur, the whole dried juice of sugarcane, is a biomass of many nutrients, including minerals, vitamins, fats, carbohydrates and protein, among others. Once pure sucrose $(C_{12}H_{22}O_{11})_n$ is extracted, it becomes potentially harmful, as shown by Prof. Brekhman's studies. In an experiment with three groups of rats: one group was fed gur alone, the second group was fed an ordinary laboratory diet, and the third group was fed sucrose alone. The group of rats fed gur alone had the longest life span. Sucrose, a single-chemical substance used everyday all over the world, can decrease the life span and is inferior to gur, a nutrient-rich substance containing unrefined sugar. Furthermore, in his personal experience with prolonged use of gur in place of ordinary sugar, Brekhman found that his memory improved considerably (Brekhman, 1983).

Whole plant materials (including roots, stems and leaves) often contain biologically active substances, which coexist in a balanced, natural way, and act quite differently on the body than any of the isolated constituents.

Side effect from different constituents being "balanced out"

Medicinal effects resulting from a cooperative action of the constituents

Fig. 9 : Various herbal components interacting harmoniously without negative side effects

The chemically pure substance reserpine[F16], an alkaloid extracted from the herb *Rauwolfia serpentina* (*Sarpgandha* in Hindi), produced toxic side effects including gastric and duodenal ulcers and suicidal tendencies in some patients who were treated with this drug for arterial hypertension and psychosis. In Ayurveda, the crude whole root of *Rauwolfia serpentina* has been used for its tranquilizing and hypotensive effects since before the times of Carak and Susrut (2700 to 600 BC) and is still used today without these adverse side effects. Another example is *morphine*, an alkaloid derived from opium, which is used in modern medicine for analgesia and sedation. It constricts the smooth muscles of the gall bladder, which may cause biliary colic, as well as constricting intestinal sphincter, which often results in severe constipation. This effect is markedly less when the whole substance opium is used because of *papaverine*, another alkaloid present in opium, which counteracts the effect of morphine through smooth muscle relaxant activity.

Tridosha concept and medicinal uses of Tulsi in Ayurveda

In Ayurveda, disease is seen from a holistic point of view as a disturbance of normal physiological functions of the body. Tulsi is considered a regulator of the three *doshas* (disharmonies of the physiological functions of the body).

Tridosha means the "three defects" in the body systems. These systems are *vata* (or *vayu*), *pitta* and *kapha*, meaning literally "wind", "bile" and "phlegm", and are often referred to as "air", "fire" and "water" respectively. They are actually three primary principles controlling the functions of the body, comprising the biomotor force, the metabolic activity and the preservative principle. In our interpretation, the first, vata is related to energy formation and conservation, tissue respiration and related mechanisms. The second, pitta is related to the enzymes and neurohumoral systems (neurological system and its related hormones). The third, kapha is related to water and electrolyte balance. A predominance of one dosha suppressing the others, results in a disease related to that particular system of the body. For example, if there is predominance in kapha, a disease of imbalance of water and electrolytes will occur. A similar interpretation has been expressed by a prominent vaidya in the *Materia Medica of Ayurveda* (Dash and Kashyap, 2000). Our extensive search in the available classic texts of Ayurveda has failed to uncover a definitive delineation of the doshas, although literature concerning tridosha-related diseases is available in plenty.

[F16] In many countries, reserpine is not used any longer because of its side effects.

Tulsi contains many bioactive substances, including minerals and vitamins, which normalize the disturbed physiological functions of the body by harmonizing the different imbalances (energy formation/conservation and tissue respiration, neurological system and neurohormones and water/electrolyte system). This general regulating faculty of Tulsi is consistent with the ancient Ayurvedic concept of the tridoshas. The ancient texts of Ayurveda describe the multiple uses of Tulsi in many human disorders, as is clearly laid down in the following Sanskrit verses:

हिक्काकासविषश्वासपार्श्वशूल विनाशनः ।
पित्तकृत्कफवातघ्नः सुरसः पूतिगन्धहा ।।
(चरक सूत्र 27/164)

Tulsi has been described by *Carak* to be useful in hiccups, coughs, poisoning, respiratory diseases, backaches and arthritis induced by pitta. (Carak Sutra 27/164)

क्फानिलविषश्वासकासदौर्गन्ध्यनाशनः ।
पित्तकृत्पार्श्वशूलघ्नः सुरसः समुदाहृतः ।।
(सुश्रुत सूत्र 46/234)

Susrut earlier has described Tulsi's usefulness in treating impotence, poisoning, dyspnea, coughs and halitosis. Backaches induced by pitta are treated by fresh, succulent leaves of Tulsi. (Susrut Sutra 46/234)

तुलसी लघुरुष्णा च रूक्षा कफविनाशिनी ।
कृमिदोषं निहन्त्येषा रुचिकृद् वह्निदीपनी ।।
(धन्वन्तरि निघन्टु)

Dhanvantari Nighantu describes Tulsi to be energy inducing and non-unctuous, antiparasitic, digestion enhancing and curative of coughs.

तुलसी कटुका तिक्त हृद्योष्ठा दाहपित्तकृत् ।
दीपनी कुष्ठकृच्छ्रास्रपार्श्वरुक्कफवातजित् ।।
शुक्ला कृष्णा च तुलसी गुणैस्तुल्या प्रकीर्त्तिता ।।
(भाव प्रकाश)

Bhavprakash describes Tulsi to be hot, bitter and useful in heartburn induced by vitiated pitta. It is a digestive and useful in urinary tract infections with burning, backaches, coughs, arthritis and other diseases induced by vitiated vata. Further, Tulsi varieties with either purple/blackish leaves (*Krishna*) or green leaves (*Rama*) have similar properties.

The *Ayurvedic Pharmacopoeia* (Singh, 1983), describes the following Ayurvedic characteristics of Tulsi:

Guna *(property of an Ayurvedic herb):*
laghu (light, easily digestible) and *ruksha* (non-unctuous)

Rasa *(taste):*
katu (acrid) and *tikta* (bitter)

Vipaka *(process of digestion and assimilation or metabolism):*
katu (acrid)

Virya *(potency):*
ushna (energy-inducing)

Karma *(action/effect):*
Antipyretic, anti-inflammatory, blood purifying, antiparasitic, insect repellent, digestive, anticough, deodorant, diuretic.

Tulsi is also used as a vehicle (anupana) to improve the efficacy of many Ayurvedic preparations.

The herbal preparations listed in Table 2 contain Tulsi leaves, amongst other herbs, as described in the *Ayurvedic Pharmacopoeia* (Anonymous, 1820).

Table 2. Ayurvedic herbal preparations containing Tulsi

Ayurvedic preparation	Application (Medical terms are explained in the glossary)
Anupanas	For fevers (antipyretic), bronchial asthma, bronchitis, coryza, pulmonary tuberculosis
Cwasahara	For bronchial asthma
Surasa	For bronchial asthma, bronchitis, cough, catarrh, loss of appetite
Mahajwarankuca Rasa	For fevers
Jwarakunjana - parindra Rasa	For fevers, bronchial asthma, cough, dysentery, general weakness, gonorrhea, jaundice
Citaria Rasa	For chronic fevers
Bhallataka Lauha	For abdominal pains, dysentery, gonorrhea, intestinal worms, piles, loss of appetite, *thinness of semen, weakness, and premature aging*
Bhaktavipaka Bati	For loss of appetite, fever and constipation
Dakamuladya Ghrita	For bronchial asthma
Lauha Parppati	For anemia, bronchial asthma and general debility
Vrihat Yogaraja Guggulu	For arthritis
Saurecwara Ghrita	For diarrhea due to giardiasis or amebiasis, filariasis, goitre, hernias, tubercular lymph nodes, tumors
Rasacekhara Cwitrapanchanana oil	For abscesses, boils, syphilis, tuberculoid leprosy, leucoderma (to be applied locally)
Durlabha Rasa	For boils
Mahanila oil	For headaches (topically, as a drink or snuff), premature greying of hair
Vakuladya oil	For loose teeth (as a snuff or mouth lotion)
Maktadi Mahanjana	For eye diseases (topically)
Kumara Kalyana Ghrita	For ailments that appear during teething in children

Furthermore, it is described that the expressed juice of fresh Tulsi leaves is used in chronic fevers, hemorrhage, dysentery and dyspepsia.

Tulsi's profertile effect in Ayurveda

The Ayurvedic literature offers much praise for Tulsi's profertile effects in both men and women. The ancient texts, such as *Susruta Samhita* (Susruta Sutra 46/234), *Padmapurana* and *Garudapurana*, written after many centuries of observation of Tulsi use, describe the herb as a *childgiver* and great *spermatogenic agent*, increasing the production of sperm (Vedvyasa, 1960; Vedavyasa, 1964; Shastri, 1968). They report that Tulsi is a *fertility improver* and enhances the chances of women bearing progeny. The Ayurvedic preparation arishtha aasav, containing five parts of Tulsi plant, jaggery, pepper and acacia bark is used to treat deficiencies of semen, such as low sperm count and thinness. Laghu raajmrigank, another Ayurvedic formulation containing Tulsi, is reported to be useful in treating problems of infertility due to abnormalities of the semen or of the menstrual cycle resulting from excess of vata (Rai, 1988).

Ayurveda and modern scientific medicine

Limitations of modern research techniques in Ayurvedic medicine

For millennia, Ayurvedic physicians have observed the effects of various plant, animal and mineral medicines, documenting thier actions and giving information for their safe medical use. As noted previously, while modern scientific techniques may provide useful data, the long-standing holistic approach of Ayurveda through natural medicines cannot be simply superseded by modern methods. The result of relatively short-term animal studies and human clinical trials are typically variable and often limited in their general applicability. Furthermore, the experienced physician's own perceptions about the effectiveness of a treatment cannot be simply displaced by out-of-context research. As humans are physically, mentally and emotionally very complex, in many respects the observations made by the ancient physicians over prolonged periods of time may provide a more accurate overall assessment of the effect of herbal medicine than short-term clinical studies and experiments.

The generalizability of laboratory experiments and human clinical studies to practical therapeutic application is always limited, as such research can never be completely standardized nor fully reflect the natural human condition. As individuals and conditions are never completely alike, the effect of drugs will not be exactly the same from application to application – even with double blind, placebo-controlled designs[F17], in spite of their increased reproducibility and validity.

Limitations of animal research

Inter-species generalizations require considerable caution and further empirical validation must be obtained before the results of animal studies can be directly applied to humans. As noted by Laurence, (1997), animal studies do not necessarily predict similar

---

[F17] Double-blind, placebo controlled study: Comparison of two groups of subjects that are subjected to different treatment regimes: experimental and control. The experimental group is administered the treatment of interest while the *control group* is given a placebo (a substance without relevant pharmacological activity, but with the appearance of the real drug). Wherever possible, subjects should be allocated randomly to their respective groups. Neither the investigators nor the patient/subjects are aware of which treatment is allocated to which subject until after the data has been collected and analyzed (double-blind trial). This procedure reduces the possible influence of subjective biases and environmental influences distorting the findings.

effects in humans.:

"The use of animals would be totally unjustified if results useful to man could not be obtained. In many known respects, animals are similar to man, but in many respect they are not. Increasingly, the low-prediction tests are being defined and eliminated. Knowledge of the mode of action of a potential new drug obviously greatly enhances prediction from animal studies of what will happen in man. Whenever practicable such knowledge should be obtained; sometimes this is quite easy, but sometimes it is impossible."

Clearly, the results of studies of one species cannot be automatically transferred to another—the validity of any such generalization must be independently demonstrated. Research on opium and opium-receptors in the brain provides an example. The administration of opium to different species gives very different results. In the case of cats, opium results in aggressive behavior and dilated pupils of the eye, while with most other mammals, including humans, sedated behavior and constricted pupils occur. Studies on cannabis effects on animal and human lung cells offer another example. "While control culture of normal animal (mouse) cells disclose rather frequently a spontaneous malignant transformation, those of normal human cells do not show spontaneous malignant transformations" (Leuchtenberger and Leuchtenberger 1972). Furthermore, our investigations of humans smoking ganja (flowering tops of female cannabis plant) for a period of 8-25 years did not show any change in their lung cytology (Singh *et al.*, 1981).

It is often extremely difficult to determine the relevance of the drug doses and treatment schedules used in animal experiments to likely human doses and patterns of use. Often, very high doses and extreme conditions are employed in animal research, which may have little practical human applications. In addition, animal studies frequemtly involve administration modes (e.g., injection) and dosage forms (e.g., extracts or isolates) that are not likely to be commonly employed in human use.

While the benefits of Tulsi have been documented in humans for millennia, most of the modern research has been done on animals. With very few exceptions, the animal studies have tended to corroborate and confirm the related claims in Ayurvedic literature, and are in general agreement with the findings of modern human research and clinical experience with Tulsi. Future research emphasis must be placed on direct human investigation.

Comparison of Ayurveda and modern allopathic drug treatment

Ayurveda and modern science can work very well together. Rishi Atreya, the supreme physician in the book of Carak, states that Ayurvedic knowledge and medicine evolve continually for the benefit of all life. In this sense, Ayurvedic medicine continues to adapt in modern times and is compatible with ongoing scientific research.

सोऽनन्तपारं त्रिस्कन्धामायुर्वेदम् ।

(चरक सूत्र 1/25)

न चैव ह्यस्ति सुतरमायुर्वेदस्य पारम् ।

(चरक सूत्र 7/14)

In the above sloka Carak states: "Ayurvedic knowledge is unrestricted and open to development."

However, as noted earlier the Ayurvedic approach is a *holistic* one, contrary to the common modern medical approach. In allopathic medicine, a particular aspect of the patient is typically treated with an isolated compound or a synthetic drug (or combinations thereof), most commonly attempting to target a specific receptor in the body to bring about the desired effect. As specific as the chemical substance may be, its over all effects on the human body are still broad. For example, oral synthetic antidiabetics act on the Islets of Langerhans in the pancreas to increase the secretion of insulin and may induce hypoglycemia by exaggerated pharmacological effect, which in turn may produce generalized symptoms of tachycardia, arterial hypertension, perspiration and even coma.

Ayurvedic herbs contain *a great many complex biochemical substances*. As noted earlier, the overall medicinal impact is the result of a cooperative interaction of the various constituents, which may have a salutary, desired medicinal effect without inducing negative side effects or toxicity (Singh *et al.,* 1993). Isolated chemicals, on the other hand, may be more potent in a specific manner, but are foreign to the human system, and are often more readily toxic. We generally advocate the use of whole herbs in their naturally existing biomass and balanced biochemical system, rather than the use of isolated active constituents.

Improving human health and increasing resistance to disease through herbal medicine and nutrition is typically slow but highly effective. Certain health-promoting herbs are naturally compatible with the human body and humans have used them for many thousands of years, for both nutrition and medicine.[F18] Medicinal substances present in the herbs tend to be *easily assimilated* into the human body; their bioavailability is typically much higher than that of single chemical substances that are foreign to the body. For example, synthetic iron preparations, used to treat anemia, are difficult for the body to assimilate compared with organic iron of herbal origin. When treated with Ayurvedic processes, iron, zinc, gold and other metals become more beneficial and easily absorbed. Such special mineral preparations, made through prolonged heating and cooling procedures, are called *bhasmas* (Nand, 1973).

Many Ayurvedic herbs have a *long-term, subtle effect on the physiological functions* of the human body and can normalize the altered physiological functions of the sick body over time. Modern drugs, however, tend to have a relatively strong impact, which may result in severe dysfunction in certain applications. For example, prednisone and acetylsalicylic acid (aspirin) may induce ulcers of the stomach. In spite of the impression of specificity, drugs have general pharmacological effects, the extent of which is not fully known. Sometimes the body reacts with hypersensitivity to a substance, in which case an allergic shock can occur, which could be fatal. For example, the anticoagulant effect of acetylsalicylic acid may be exaggerated in some individuals, resulting

---

[F18] In ancient times, some Ayurvedic treatments included not only medicinal herbs but also a protein-rich diet from wild animal sources, in combination with nutritious local fruits and plants. In those days the Indian subcontinent was covered with large forests, where wild animals and natural herbs existed in abundance. Nowhere have Ayurvedic textbooks recommended the use of meat of domesticated animals, as in modern society. Wild animals are scarce nowadays; farmed animals are generally less healthy and can be carriers of different diseases (such as 'mad-cow-disease' or cysticercosis, caused by *Taenia solium*) and are typically chemically contaminated with hormones and antibiotics. Therefore, most modern Ayurvedic physicians recommend pulses, grains and dairy products as sources of protein.

in severe hemorrhage and death, due to thrombocytopenia (Laurence, 1997). Another example is the allergic reaction to penicillin, which can result in anaphylactic shock and interstitial nephritis (Tierney *et al.,* 1995).

Herbal remedies may also have potential side effects, yet, as noted above, they often possess balancing components that both minimize these effects and add to the range and spectrum of their therapeutic usefulness. Ayurvedic herbs in appropriate dosages are generally innocuous. Furthermore, many of these herbs are health tonics, as they also possess nutrient qualities and have health-promoting and antiaging properties. Synthetic drugs generally do not act as nutrients. Some even enhance the process of aging (e.g., certain nonsteroidal anti-inflammatories such as ibuprofen).

In Ayurveda, the learned rishis (Carak school) have said that there is no substance on earth that cannot be used as a medicine, depending on the circumstances. This even includes cobra venom and rocks.

नानौषधिभूतं जगति किन्चिद् द्रव्यमुपलभ्यते ।
(सुश्रुत सूत्र 26)

In the above sloka Sushrut states: "By interconnectedness of all life, all substances are medicine in various conditions of health and disease."

Combining Ayurvedic herbs and allopathic drugs

In modern times, Ayurveda can provide a *supplement* to synthetic drugs and other modern treatments, reducing their negative impact. For example, by destroying beneficial bacteria, antibiotic treatment induces depletion of vitamins and minerals by rendering their intestinal absorption incomplete. Herbal preparations may help to replace these nutrients and support the growth of healthy intestinal flora, as well as being intestinal soothing agents.

Ayurveda can also be used as a *complementary* medicine, augmenting or enhancing the beneficial effects of allopathic medicine. For example, Ayurvedic antidiabetic preparations reduce the needed dosage of insulin or synthetic oral antidiabetics and can help in better control of diabetes mellitus (Pushpangadan and Sobti, 1977; Agarwal *et al.,* 1995).

In addition, Ayurveda can be the *medicine of first choice* for long-term treatment in many chronic ailments like diabetes mellitus, bronchial asthma, arthritis, tumors, cardiovascular diseases (arterial hypertension, myocardial infarction etc.), allergies and others, where a mild form of the disease is found. As a complement to the long term Ayurvedic treatment, synthetic drugs can be appropriately used from time to time, as needed, when acute exacerbation of the chronic disease occurs.

Comparative development of herbal and allopathic medicines

The research development process of modern synthetic drugs is very different from that of ancient herbal medicines.

Modern drugs are usually initially unknown substances, which are first tested for possible positive and negative effects on "biological models" using animals, before being cautiously subjected to exploratory human clinical trials. Even if these results are positive, the full effects and potential dangers of general use of the new medicines cannot be accurately predicted. Examples of major errors in the screening of modern drugs include the

Thalidomide tragedy and the Occulo-mucocutaneous syndrome of Proctolol. Only one new drug out of thousands is finally considered applicable for general human use.

In the case of Ayurvedic herbal medicines, which are complex natural biochemical substances that have been used holistically and studied for centuries, the process is the reverse. With ancient herbs like Tulsi and Neem (*Azadirachta indica*) our main task is to authenticate already well-known human therapeutic uses through experiments and clinical trial/assessments. We do not need to start from scratch with exploratory animal experiments, although it has become customary to conduct animal toxicity studies, as are done for modern medicines. However, this is often not very informative, nor necessary because the general lack of toxicity of the herbs is already very well known. Therefore, our primary focus is on confirming the traditional medicinal and nutritional values of such herbs in modern human application. Once the therapeutic value is authenticated by current scientific means, the herbs can assume a role in modern medical practice.

Figure 10 depicts the evaluation and development of medicines of Ayurvedic herbal origin compared to that of modern synthetic agents. The positive and negative oscillations in the phases of development of many modern drugs, as described by Laurence *et al.* (1997), are depicted on the right side of the figure 10. To start, (1) A new drug posed as an innovative treatment idea, (2) which, if successful, may become accepted as a wonder drug, and (3) then toxic effects typically appear, which send the drug back to the lowest level. Next, (4) more cautious use may find it to be effective therapy under certain conditions in a particular disease.

Over the centuries, unscientific practitioners have sometimes distorted descriptions of the proper Ayurvedic use of certain herbs in different diseases and conditions. Hence the need for validating alleged benefits. For example, hardly any of the herbs often claimed to be useful in the treatment of snake poisoning have been scientifically shown to have significant therapeutic effect (Kirtikar and Basu, 1935). As 85% of snakes in India are non-poisonous, certain physicians may have had apparent success in such cases and achieved a reputation of curing snakebites, complete with back-up testimonials from the patients who, in fact, may have received non-poisonous bites and been treated with placebos lacking any relevant pharmacological action. Furthermore, in some Ayurvedic books, it appears that almost every herb can be used to treat all kinds of diseases. (See Vaidyaratnam P.S. Varier's *Indian Medicinal Plants, Vol. 1-5,* 1994-1996.) It is important to determine what in the rich resource of Ayurvedic texts are the valid treatments.

With the advances in biotechnological methods, scientific herbal medicines can be effectively employed for the safe treatment of many human diseases now and in the future. Modern medicine is evolving towards a holistic approach and the potential contribution of Ayurveda to the healthy future of humanity is clearly evident. Ayurveda is a time-tested, holistic approach for the preservation of health and the prevention and cure of diseases, and has much to offer. As a broad science of life, it also provides knowledge for the most harmonious coexistence of human life and the environment. We contend that modernized Ayurveda should provide the foundation of

Ayurvedic Medicines

Complex bioactive substances, mainly from herbs clinically used for centuries and considered nontoxic. Studies desired.

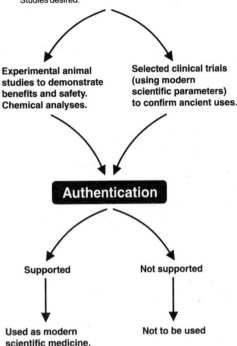

Modern Synthetic Medicines

Generally chemicals of unknown properties and toxicity. In some cases chemical structure-related properties are partially predicted. Out of thousands tried, few are determined fit for human use.

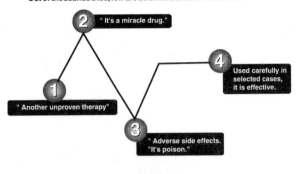

1. New drug (thought to be unreliable)
2. Becomes popular as wonderful cure
3. Adverse effects appear and use fails.
4. More studies reveal that when used carefully it is good for certain diseases (stable line).

Oscillations in the development of some drugs
(Laurence et al., 1997)

Possible mode of development of Ayurvedic Herbs
(Dr. N. Singh)

Fig 10 : *Proposed development of Ayurvedic drugs as compared to modern synthetic drugs*

the medicine of the future (Singh, 1986a, Singh, 1986c). Recent findings of the chromosomal studies of Tusli like X=8 and X=12 in Basilicum and Sanctum groups respectively, further enhances the validity of holistic approach of Ayurveda (Bansi *et al.*, 2000).

Stress in Human Health and Disease

Stress and the General Adaptation Syndrome

In 1950, Selye defined stress as the "sum of all non-specific changes caused by function or damage in the human organism" (Selye, 1950). Stress in itself is a natural response of the body to stimuli, the primary objective of which is to maintain life and to homeostatically re-establish the normal state of the organism. If the stimulus persists for a long time or if it is of severe intensity, it may manifest in a variety of diseases, depending on the genetic predisposition of the individual, as well as a variety of interacting environmental and experiential factors. The stress may be physical (e.g., cold or heat), chemical (e.g., pollution and drugs), biological (e.g., bacterial or viral infections), emotional (e.g., anger and grief) or circumstantial (e.g., divorce, moving residence or taking an exam) (Selye, 1971). Selye was the first to distinguish three stages of stress in what he identified as the *General Adaptation Syndrome* (GAS), through which the body adapts itself while in a state of stress.

These stages consist of:

1. Alarm
2. Resistance or adaptation to stress
3. Exhaustion

The initial alarm triggers the body's natural defensive mechanisms. Failure of adaptation leads to the third stage, exhaustion, which may result in disease or even death. Among its many possible adverse consequences, stress can increase the vulnerability of an organism to certain diseases by exerting an immunosuppressive effect — especially diseases associated with immunological mechanisms, such as infections, malignomas and autoimmune diseases (Singh *et al.*, 1982). The persistent and excessive stress of modern life and the explosion of new therapeutic drugs in allopathic medicine (i.e., chemical stressors) have brought an epidemic of a new form of disorders that are not necessarily infectious, which we call *stress-related diseases* (Bhargava and Singh, 1981; Singh, 1981; Bhargava and Singh, 1984; Bhargava and

Singh, 1985). Among them are myocardial infarction, atherosclerosis, arterial hypertension, cancer, diabetes mellitus, rheumatoid arthritis, bronchial asthma, gastric and duodenal ulcers and more (Papov, 1975; Singh and Misra, 1987).

Stress activates the *hypothalamo-pituitary(hypophyseal)-adrenal axis*[F19] (HPA), which plays a central role in the adaptation of the organism to stress. In addition, there are other mechanisms involving hormones and enzymes, which help the adaptive process (Ramasarma, 1978).

Adaptogen/antistress agents

It has been found that certain herbs induce a *State of Non-specific Increased Resistance* of the organism to stress (called SNIR or adaptogenic property). Agents improving the capability of the organism to adapt to stressors are called *adaptogens*[F20]. The concept of adaptogens as a separate group of

medicinal substances was first developed by Lazarev (1958) to describe an agent that helps return the balance of altered physiological functions of the body to the normal state. In medical applications we call these adaptogens *antistress agents*[F21] emphasizing their therapeutic pharmacological action.

An ideal *adaptogen/antistress* agent must fulfill three requirements:

- it must be innocuous in nature;
- it must have a normalizing action on the physiological functions of the body;
- it must induce a State of Non-specifically Increased Resistance (SNIR) of the human organism, so that the body copes better with stress.

Herbs that contain this adaptogenic property help the individual to cope with stress more successfully. Aging is closely related to changes in stress reactivity and to decrease of adaptation capacity. This loss in

---

[F19] There exists a reciprocal communication between the brain and endocrine system on one side and the immune system on the other. This is fundamental for the defense mechanism of the human organism. The integration of a broad spectrum of stimuli happens in the hypothalamus, a brain region. Through a releasing hormone the hypothalamus acts on the pituitary gland, which releases ACTH. ACTH acts on the adrenal glands and stimulates the synthesis and secretion of glucocorticoids and adrenaline. The glucocorticoids act in a feedback mechanism on the hypothalamus and pituitary gland and regulate the release of the hormones and thereby contain the responses of the adrenal glands to stress within appropriate limits (Fulder, 1981). In the hypothalamo-pituitary-adrenal (HPA) axis, the end products are the glucocorticoids with the control role of the immune/inflammatory cell function. The HPA enables the organism to adapt to diverse noxious stimuli, whether emotional, physical trauma or immune insults. It is activated in times of stress and the glucocorticoids released into the blood circulation serve to restore the balance through multiple mechanisms, which include modulation of immune/inflammatory response (Buckingham, 1996). Variation of the appropriate response (for example, excessive secretion of glucocorticoids due to stress) can cause disturbances in HPA function, immunosuppression and, in turn, predisposition to a variety of diseases like infections and cancer. Furthermore, glucocorticoids can cause gastric and duodenal ulcers, and adrenaline can produce arterial hypertension and contribute to the genesis of stress-induced diseases. Insufficient secretion of the glucocorticoids implicates a vulnerability to stress and leads to autoimmune, inflammatory and allergic disorders like rheumatoid arthritis.

[F20] Adaptogens - Substances that have a balancing and tonifying effect on the body and different systems within the body. They increase the body's ability to withstand stress, increase mental alertness, and enhance the body's performance under a wide variety of stressful conditions. Adaptogens support the non-specific immunological resistance of a person to help maintain good health, vitality and resist stress (induce a state of nonspecifically increased resistance = SNIR).

[F21] Antistress agents - preventing or reducing the ill effects of stress; a pharmacological term coined by Dr. N. Singh and co-workers. The term antistress is generally equivalent to *adaptogen* but conveys more specific relationship to medicinal effects. *Adaptogen* conveys a physiological concept, while *antistress* implies a pharmacological therapeutic property (which is adaptogenic).

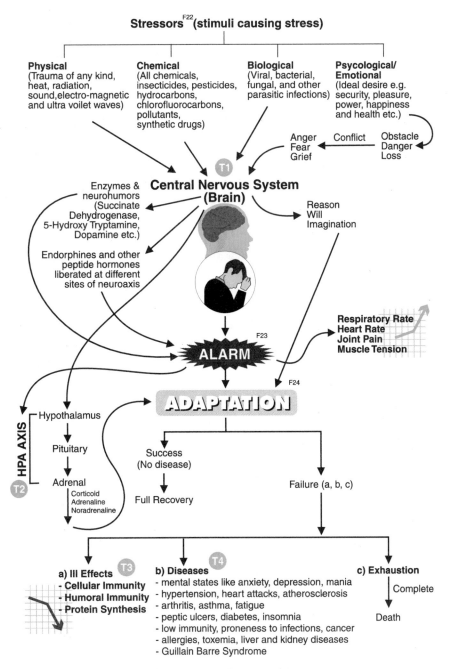

Stressors[F22] **(stimuli causing stress)**

Physical
(Trauma of any kind, heat, radiation, sound,electro-magnetic and ultra voilet waves)

Chemical
(All chemicals, insecticides, pesticides, hydrocarbons, chlorofluorocarbons, pollutants, synthetic drugs)

Biological
(Viral, bacterial, fungal, and other parasitic infections)

Psycological/ Emotional
(Ideal desire e.g. security, pleasure, power, happiness and health etc.)

Anger Fear Grief ← Conflict ← Obstacle Danger Loss

(T1) **Central Nervous System (Brain)**

Enzymes & neurohumors (Succinate Dehydrogenase, 5-Hydroxy Tryptamine, Dopamine etc.)

Reason Will Imagination

Endorphines and other peptide hormones liberated at different sites of neuroaxis

Respiratory Rate Heart Rate Joint Pain Muscle Tension

ALARM [F23]

ADAPTATION [F24]

HPA AXIS

Hypothalamus
↓
Pituitary
↓
Adrenal
Corticoid Adrenaline Noradrenaline

(T2)

Success (No disease)
↓
Full Recovery

Failure (a, b, c)

a) Ill Effects (T3)
- **Cellular Immunity**
- **Humoral Immunity**
- **Protein Synthesis**

b) Diseases (T4)
- mental states like anxiety, depression, mania
- hypertension, heart attacks, atherosclerosis
- arthritis, asthma, fatigue
- peptic ulcers, diabetes, insomnia
- low immunity, proneness to infections, cancer
- allergies, toxemia, liver and kidney diseases
- Guillain Barre Syndrome

c) Exhaustion
Complete
↓
Death

Fig 11 : Stress-disease phenomena
Possible sites (T1-T4) of Tulsi in adaptogenic/antistress action during G.A.S.[F25]

[F22] Stressors are noxious Physical, Chemical, Biological, Emotional and other stimuli which cause stress phenomenon.

[F23] Alarm is caused by the perception of danger.

[F24] Adaptation is a phenomenon of coping with and developing resistance to stress.

[F25] G.A.S. (General Adaptation Syndrome): The reaction of organism to stress is in three stages: (1) alarm, (2) adaptation or resistance, and (3) exhaustion. If the organism copes effectively, it recovers. If not, it can develop stress-related diseases, and if exhaustion is fully manifested, the organism may die.

adaptive ability results from a progressive decrease in self-regulatory mechanisms. It is possible to help the optimal functioning of these processes by pharmacological influence, and thus stem the advance of aging (Kumar *et al.,* 1982). Brekhman and Dordymov (1969) studied various medicinal plants of South Asian countries and found antistress/adaptogenic properties in many. We have conducted studies on numerous Indian and other Asian plants, demonstrating antistress/adaptogenic effects (Singh and Singh, 1978; Singh *et al.,* 1982; Srivastava *et al.,* 1984; Singh, 1984; Singh, 1986b; Jogetia *et al.,* 1986; Singh, 1993). Among these herbs, we have found Tulsi to be the superior most adaptogen.

Figure 11 depicts, in simplified form, the concepts of stress, stress disease and possible sites (T1, T2, T3 and T4) of Tulsi's adaptogenic/antistress effects.

Tulsi Research of Dr. Narendra Singh's Team

As described earlier, Tulsi is considered a main pillar of Ayurvedic herbal medicine and was long ago included in worship to ensure that all people regularly consumed it and received its benefits in their daily life. The ancient sages obviously knew that Tulsi is a vitalizing, adaptogen/antistress agent, helping humans to live a healthier and longer life. Accordingly, we selected Tulsi for specific clinical and experimental studies to explore and document its potency and usefulness as a herbal medicine for modern times. The first seicentific documentation of the antistress/adaptogenic activity of Tulsi was provided by our research group in 1978 (Singh *et al.*, 1978). Since then we have conducted studies on numerous other medicinal plants and have found Tulsi to be the best adaptogen overall (Singh and Singh, 1978; Singh, 1981; Bhargava and Singh, 1981, 1985; Singh *et al.*, 1982; Das *et al.*, 1983; Singh, 1986; Singh, 1993). A summary of our research is given below.

Animal Studies

General antistress/adaptogenic activity

The importance of Tulsi plant as a medicinal herb became more evident after the discovery of its antistress activity (Singh *et al.*, 1977a, 1977b, 1978). To evaluate the relative antistress potential of Ayurvedic herbs, 50 Indian medicinal plants were screened, and five were found to possess significant adaptogenic activity. These were compared to the popular *Panax ginseng* (Chinese ginseng) and are listed in order of their antistress potency: (1) *Ocimum sanctum* (Tulsi), (2) *Withania somnifera* (Ashwagandha)[F26], (3) *Altingia excelsa* (Silaras), (4) *Diospyros perigrina* (Kakatendu), (5) *Panax ginseng* (Chinese ginseng) and (6) *Picrorrhiza kurroa* (Katuki) (Bhargava and Singh, 1981; Singh, 1986b).

When mice are subjected to a period of prolonged swimming, a state of physical stress is induced. Among other reactions, the weight

---

[F26] Ashwagandha is sometimes referred to as *Indian ginseng*. The adaptogenic property of ashwagandha was discovered by Dr. Narendra Singh. (Singh, *el al.*, 1976 and 1982).

of the adrenal glands increases and the content of ascorbic acid and cortisol decreases. These stress-induced changes are reversed in identical conditions when pre-treatment with Tulsi is performed, even with a minimal oral dose of 10mg/kg of leaf extract (approximately equivalent to 100mg of fresh Tulsi leaves). In a follow-up experiment, we demonstrated that even in adrenalectomized animals (where the adrenal glands are removed by surgery). Tulsi increased swimming performance, indicating that the adrenal glands are not the sole site of Tulsi's adaptogenic effects. (Singh and Singh, 1978; Bhargava and Singh, 1981; Srivastava *et al.,* 1984; Singh, 1986; Singh and Misra, 1993).

Tulsi prevents adverse stress-induced, biochemical changes in the brains of mice and rats (Dixit *et al.,*1986; Misra *et al.,* 1987; Singh *et al.,* 1991a). During prolonged stress, the levels of the neurotransmitters epinephrine (adrenaline) and norepinephrine (noradrenaline) are decreased, while dopamine and 5-hydroxytryptamine (serotinin) are increased. Tulsi normalizes and balances these changes during stress by increasing epinephrine and norepinephrine in the brain, further increasing the level of dopamine (which is needed as a precursor for the synthesis of epinephrine and norepine-phrine), and inhibiting the increase 5-hydroxytryptamine.

Further exploration revealed that Tulsi assists the formation of the enzyme *succinate dehydrogenase (SDH)* in the brain of rats (Kalsi *et al.,* 1987). SDH is a mitochondrial enzyme that is activated in times of stress and assists the *formation and conservation of energy in cells* during the *Kreb's cycle,* the major metabolic pathway for generating cellular energy. SDH

helps the organism to adapt better during stress and is also known to provide defense against free radicals (Robbins *et al.,* 1982).

Tulsi increases the body's capacity to utilize oxygen. It reduces the requirement of oxygen for survival in mice; the animals are able to survive longer in hermetically sealed vessels with Tulsi, and tolerance to anoxic stress to the brain (as reflected by anoxic convulsions) was improved. O*cimum sanctum* is superior to the other varieties of Tulsi in anoxia tolerance (Bhargava and Singh, 1981; Singh, 1986; Singh, 1988). This property of Tulsi may be a significant factor in Tulsi's endurance-enhancing effects discussed below.

Antiulcer activity

Prolonged exposure to severely challenging conditions such as cold, immobilization and chemical stressors (e.g., acetylsalicylic acid) induces gastric ulcers in animals. A number of studies have demonstrated that pretreatment with Tulsi *markedly prevents such ulcers* (Singh and Misra, 1993; Bhargava and Singh, 1981; Singh and Singh, 1978; Bhargava and Singh, 1984; Bhargava and Singh, 1985).

To differentiate between general sedative and specific antiulcer activity we investigated (in rats) the effects of benzodiazepine tranquillizers (e.g., *diazepam, oxazepam, nitrazepam*) and Tulsi (aqueous extract) at different oral doses. Performance on the rota-rod test and the incidence of immobilization stress-induced ulcers were assessed. The rota-rod test is considered a sensitive measure of the sedation potential of a drug. The lower the rota-rod ED_{50}, the greater the general sedative action. ED_{50} values in both tests were calculated and the *therapeutic index* (Rota rod ED_{50}/Antiulcer ED_{50}) of each was determined, as shown in Table 3.

Table 3. *Antagonism of stress-ulcers and sedative action of benzodiazepines and Ocimum sanctum*

Drugs	Antiulcer ED_{50} ± S.E. (mg/kg p.o.)			Rota Rod ED_{50} ± S.E. (mg/kg p.o.)			Therapeutic Index Rota Rod ED_{50} /Antiulcer ED_{50}
Diazepam	9.9	±	0.01	18.7	±	0.01	1.88
Oxazepam	5.8	±	0.03	8.4	±	0.2	1.43
Nitrazepam	2.2	±	0.06	3.9	±	0.25	1.8
Ocimum Sanctum	12.3	±	1.01	255.5	±	13.9*	20.8

Benzodiazepine tranquillizers have an antiulcer effect as a result of their sedative/antianxiety action. In contrast, Tulsi prevents such stress ulcers at low *non-sedating doses* and has mild sedative effects only at very high doses –and actually improves performance at lower doses (upto 100mg/kg). Tulsi's therapeutic index was ten times greater than benzodiazepines. Thus it is a much safer agent than these popular tranquillizers for producing antiulcer effects and being an adàptogen, also increases stamina while benzodiazepine decrease it (Figure 12).

Physical endurance and performance under stress

Tulsi has been found to significantly improve the swimming performance, physical stamina and endurance of mice (Bhargava and Singh, 1981; Singh, 1986; Saksena *et al.,* 1987). Thus,

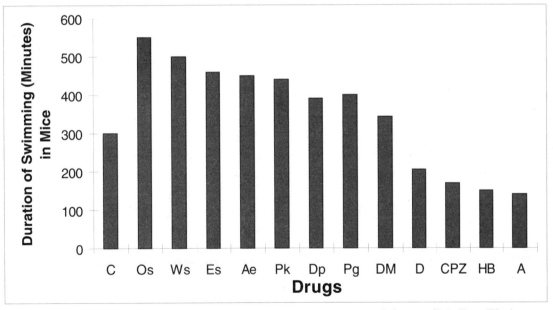

C - Normal control; **Os** - *Ocimum sanctum* (Tulsi), **Ws** - *Withania somnifera* (Ashwagandha), **Es** - *Eleutherococcus senticosus* (Siberian ginseng), **Ae** - *Altingia excelsa* (Silaras), **Pk** - *Picrorrhiza kurroa* (Katuki), **Dp** - *Diospyros perigrina* (Kakatendu), **Pg** - *Panax ginseng* (Chinese ginseng); **DM** - dexamethasone, **D** - diazepam, **CPZ** - chlorpromazine, **HB** - hexobarbitone, **A** - amphetamine.

Fig. 12. Effect of antistress plants and synthetic drugs on swimming performance

Tulsi is said to produce a *staminator* effect. A comparative study was conducted evaluating the staminator potential of a variety of herbal antistress/adaptogens, including Siberian and Chinese ginseng, and popular synthetic allopathic drugs (Singh *et al.*, 2001). Tulsi (*Ocimum sanctum*) was found to increase stamina more than any of the other herbal adaptogens, or the synthetic drugs. Tranquillizers, sedatives and stimulants markedly reduced stamina. (See Figure 12.)

As shown in Figure 12, *Ocimum sanctum*, *Withania somnifera*, *Altingia excelsa*, *Picrorrhiza kurroa*, *Diospyros perigrina*, *Eleutherococcus senticosus* and *Panax ginseng*, adaptogens/ antistress agents increased the duration of swimming time in mice as compared to the control (normal) group. Among the modern synthetic drugs, dexamethasone, diazepam, chlorpromazine, hexobarbitone and amphetamine, only dexamethasone increased the swimming time and the rest (CNS tranquillizer chlorpromazine, sedatives dexamethasone and hexobarbitone, and stimulant amphetamine) markedly reduced the duration of swimming. Dexamethasone increses endurance, but adversely affects the cardiac and other muscles by causing necrosis and, consequently cannot be safely used to increase stamina (Brekhman and Dordymov, 1969).

The potency, efficacy and toxicity of O*cimum sanctum* (Tulsi) was compared with *Eleutherococcus senticosus* (Siberian ginseng) and *Panax ginseng* (Chinese ginseng) in rat (Singh *et al.*, 1991b). We studied swimming endurance, physical stress-induced changes in adrenal gland weight, physical stress-induced decrease of ascorbic acid in the adrenal glands, and gastric ulcers induced by immobilization stress for each of the three herbs given orally

and a control group (Singh, 1986b). The dose that induced 50 percent antistress activity (ED_{50}) was determined for the four tests with each of the three herbs, and the mean ED_{50} was calculated per herb. This is called the *antistress unit* (ASU). The ASU of each herb was 14mg/kg for Tulsi, 17mg/kg for Siberian ginseng and 25mg/kg for Chinese ginseng. For comparison of relative potency, when Siberian ginseng was taken as 1, the potency of Tulsi was 1.2 and Chinese ginseng was 0.6 (Figure 13). Tulsi is 20% more potent than Siberian ginseng and is almost twice as effective as Chinese ginseng.

As noted earlier, the ratio between the LD_{50} and ED_{50} is the *safety margin* of the agent. The safety margins determined for the three herbs were: 306 for Tulsi, 242 for Siberian ginseng and 208 for Chinese ginseng, the toxicity of Tulsi is much less than that of Siberian ginseng and Chinese ginseng (Singh *et al.*, 1991b). High toxic doses of *Panax ginseng* in humans produce a corticoid-like syndrome with insomnia, restlessness, diarrhea, edema and arterial hypertension, which limits its use as a health tonic (Siegel, 1979). Such toxic symptoms are not observed with Tulsi (Bhargava and Singh, 1981), which has a better safety margin as well as higher potency. These data support the contention that Tulsi is an ideal antistress agent for long-term use in the prevention and treatment of human stress-related ailments.

Other benefits of Tulsi

Liver protective and antioxidant effects

Tulsi has been found to *protect against free radical damage* in the liver of animals and human (Singh and Singh, 1978; Bhargava and Singh, 1981; Bhargava and Singh, 1984; Singh, 1986; Singh and Misra, 1993; Mishra *et al.*, 1998).

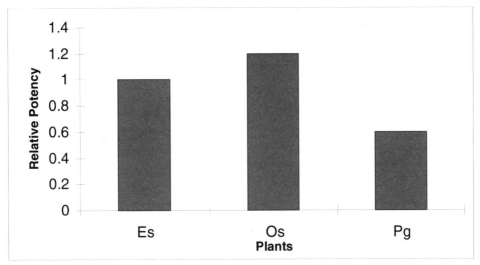

Es – *Eleutherococcus senticosus* (Siberian ginseng), **Os** – *Ocimum sanctum* (Tulsi), **Pg** – *Panax ginseng* (Chinese ginseng). Potency of **Es** is taken as 1 for comparison.

Figure 13. Relative antistress potency of three herbal adaptogens

This is a result of its *antioxidant properties*. Free radical damage was produced in this experiment by treatment with the liver-toxic chemical carbon tetrachloride (CCl_4). As CCl_4 is metabolized by the enzyme of smooth endoplasmic reticulum (SER), free radicals $CCl_3^{\bullet}$ and Cl^- are released. $CCl_3^{\bullet}$ is highly toxic to liver (Robbins *et al.*, 1982). Toxic lipid peroxidation of the cell membrane is a consequence of free radical damage and takes place in healthy tissues as well as in a number of pathological states. Tulsi has significant quantities of the well-known antioxidants, vitamins A and C, and selenium, as well as other free radical scavenging substances, including flavonoids and essential oils.

Radiation protective effects

Tulsi has significant antiradiation effect. Rats treated with Tulsi and exposed to experimental radiation have a lower mortality rate than rats in a control group. The reduction of mortality was 30 to 70 percent after seven days of treatment with 25mg/kg orally of aqueous extract of Tulsi leaves (Jogetia *et al.*, 1986). This protection is likely due, atleast in part, to the potent antioxidant effects of Tulsi.

Antidiarrheal (intestinal tract motility) effects

Tulsi was found to decrease the intestinal transit of charcoal in rats. This reduction in the rate of passage of charcoal is due to reduction of peristaltic movements (movement of the intestinal walls to transport the food material) (Singh *et al.*, 1991c).

Antiasthmatic effects

Histamine, *Acacia arabica*, *Holoptelea* and *Zea mays* provoke bronchial asthma in guinea pigs. Tulsi reduces the bronchospasms and the mortality induced by bronchospasms (Palit *et al.*, 1980; Palit *et al.*, 1983). Tulsi can play an important role in preventing and relieving asthma.

Anti-inflammatory and antipyretic effects

Tulsi has *anti-inflammatory and antipyretic (fever lowering) activities* in albino rats, and is effective in reducing both acute and chronic inflammation (Singh, 1984).

Antidiabetic effects

Tulsi was found to be effective in reducing the effects of experimental diabetes mellitus in rats (Singh and Misra, 1993).

Anabolic effects

An aqueous extract of Tulsi leaves in doses of 100mg/kg given orally for three months had an *anabolic effect* (enhancing protein synthesis) in rats, increasing the weight of the anus sphincter muscle (a method to assess anabolic activity). An increase in overall body weight also occurred and no toxic effects were detected (Singh, 1986b).

Antiaggressive, calming effects

Albino rats display aggressive behavior when subjected to audiogenic stress. Tulsi markedly reduces this aggressive behavior indicating that Tulsi has a calming effect on the central nervous system in situations of physical stress (Singh, 1986b; Singh and Misra, 1993).

Human clinical studies

Numerous human studies were carried out to explore Tulsi's capacity for the prevention and treatment of stress-related diseases. Clinical studies were undertaken in cases of bronchial asthma, viral encephalitis, stress-related arterial hypertension, compromised states of the humoral and cellular immune system, gastric ulcers, arthritis and chronic fatigue syndrome. This research which further strengthens Tulsi's traditional reputation as the "Mother Medicine of Nature" is summarized below.

Tulsi in the treatment of bronchial asthma

In our clinical trials of Tulsi effects on bronchial asthma, 500mg of dried Tulsi leaves were given to 15 patients three times per day for one month (Dixit *et al.*,1986, Singh *et al.*, 1986). There was a reduction in the eosinophil count in blood and sputum (expressing a reduction of allergic reaction), an increase in hemoglobin and an increase in body weight in the majority of the patients. The pulmonary function of the patients treated with Tulsi improved considerably: there was a reduction in frequency of spasmodic attacks, a significant reduction in breathlessness, a decrease in respiration rate, an increase in forced vital capacity, maximum breathing capacity and increased expectoration. Overall, there was a marked improvement in these patients at the end of one month. Some improvement was noticeable the first day of treatment, as the expectorant and broncho-dilator effects of Tulsi started within hours after the first ingestion.

Tulsi in the treatment of viral encephalitis

We conducted a study during an epidemic of Japanese viral encephalitis type B in Eastern U.P., India, in the months of September to November 1978 (Das *et al.*, 1983). Sixteen patients were admitted to the King George's Medical College Associated Hospitals in Lucknow. Acute viral encephalitis was diagnosed on the basis of clinical and virological studies. One group of six patients received 2.5gm of fresh Tulsi leaves four times daily, 5 were evaluated and the other group of 10 patients was kept on treatment with steroids, 8 were evaluated. For ethical reasons, no placebo control group (without administration of either treatment) was employed. The survival rate of patients in the group treated with Tulsi was significantly higher than in the group treated with steroids. Furthermore, there was a low incidence of viral neurological deficit in the patients treated with Tulsi. There was a complete recovery in 60% patients treated with Tulsi while 0% in patients treated with steroids. Usually there is a very high incidence of neurological damage with viral encephalitis. In the Tulsi group, the increased survival rate and the marked reduction in neurological deficit in the survivors are likely due to the herb's antiviral and general antistress/adaptogenic effects.

The results of this study, and the fact that Tulsi has been used in ancient Ayurvedic medicine for many viral infections, suggests that Tulsi be explored in the prevention and treatment of AIDS and other viral diseases, as discussed below.

Tulsi in the treatment of stress-related arterial hypertension

We conducted a double blind, placebo-controlled, clinical study the effect of Tulsi on mild-to-moderate arterial hypertension, where stress appeared to be a major factor (Singh 1986b; Srivastava *et al.*, 1986). In one group of 25 patients, 500mg of powdered, dried Tulsi leaves was given three times daily for a period of six weeks; whereas in the control group of 25 patients, a placebo (inactive substance) was given. Tulsi produced a significant average fall in systolic (26 mm Hg) and diastolic (16 mm Hg) blood pressure from the second week on. The hypotensive effect of Tulsi persisted for at least two weeks after withdrawal of the herb. Tulsi can be used

for long periods in the prevention and treatment of stress-related arterial hypertension, as it reduces the blood pressure smoothly to acceptable levels (in this case, to an average of 124 mm Hg systolic and 84 mm Hg diastolic) and is free from negative side effects.

Effects of Tulsi on cell-mediated and humoral immune response

If a subject is allergic to an allergen, its direct contact causes an inflammation of the skin. With certain allergens this inflammation of the skin (redness and swelling) appears after one to two days (delayed hypersensitivity). This type of allergy is called *T-cell-mediated hypersensitivity* because it is mediated by the helper T-lymphocytes (a subpopulation of the lymphocytes).

In a placebo-controlled study, dinitro-chlorobenzene (DNCB), serving as the allergen was applied on the skin of the forearm of patients for assessment of the T-cell mediated immune response (Kumar *et al.,* 1982; Singh, 1986b; Dixit and Singh, 1987). The application of DNCB results in contact sensitivity with induration and erythema of the skin an expression of the T-cellular immune response to this antigen.[F27] Tulsi was given to 20 patients for four weeks, and significantly enhanced this cell-mediated immunity (i.e., a greater number of immune defense cells were formed and the immune protective response was more marked). The property of increasing cell-mediated immune response is useful for defense against viral infections, stress and malignomas where cell-mediated immunity is reduced. Prolonged use

---

[F27] An allergy is an immunologically mediated reaction to a foreign antigen, or allergen. The DNCB sensitization is a *type IV allergic reaction* (i.e., a delayed hypersensitivity or cell-mediated immunity). Antigen specific receptors develop on T-lymphocytes (a subgroup of white blood cells, responsible for immune defense) and subsequent administration of this antigen leads to a local skin reaction or tissue allergic reaction.

of Tulsi can be particularly beneficial to elderly individuals, where a decline in normal immune response occurs – primarily due to a reduction in T-cell function of the immune system (because of thymus involution).

Tulsi may be useful in *acquired immunodeficiency syndrome (AIDS)*, where the cell-mediated immunity is markedly reduced, due to leucopenia – especially the T-lymphocytes. As the incubation time of AIDS is very long, regular use of Tulsi may prevent the manifestation of the disease by modulating the cell-mediated immunity. (See related animal studies in Chapter 6.)

Tulsi in the treatment of chronic fatigue

The staminator effect of Tulsi shown in mice led to the study of antifatigue effects in humans. One capsule of 300mg of dried, slightly crushed Tulsi leaves was given daily to 56 aging patients for a period of three months to one year, in addition to their other herbal treatment programs (addressing arterial hypertension, rheumatoid arthritis, osteoarthritis etc.). Within one week, 90 percent of the patients described a reduction of fatigue, and within one month all patients felt an improvement of fatigue symptoms. After discontinuing Tulsi, the effect lasted for more than a month. In the patients suffering from rheumatoid arthritis, an increase in body weight, hemoglobin percentage of the blood and increase in muscle power (as judged by increase of the grip strength) was observed (Singh and Abbas, 1995a–unpublished). In a follow-up placebo-controlled study, 500 mg of dried Tulsi leaves were given twice daily for three months to 27 young male Indians suffering from chronic fatigue (Singh and Abbas, 1995b). There was a significant reduction of fatigue in the patients receiving Tulsi in comparison to those on placebo.

Tulsi research of other scientists

Animal Studies

Radiation protective effect

In 1985, Dr. N. Singh delivered a lecture on various antistress plants, including Tulsi and Ashwagandha, at the Manipal Medical College Karnataka India. Afterwards, Prof. P. Uma Devi, head of the Radiobiology Department agreed to carry out radiobiology studies on Tulsi and other herbs in collaboration with us. Aqueous extracts of two varieties of *Ocimum sanctum* (Rama and Krishna Tulsi) and *Ocimum gratissimum* (Vana Tulsi) were provided to the team. All three varieties of Tulsi were shown to have significant antiradiation effect in animals, as presented at the Indian Science Congress at Jaipur in 1986 (Jogetia *et al.*, 1986).

In 1997, Uma Devi and coworkers studied bone marrow stem cell survival after gamma radiation (Ganasoundari *et al.*, 1997). Tulsi extract administered with radiotherapy gave a higher stem cell survival rate, suggesting likely good results with human clinical use. The research group also examined chromosome aberration in cells of bone marrow in irradiated mice and found radioprotective effects of two flavonoids, orientin and vicenin, obtained from the leaves of *Ocimum sanctum*. The non-toxic nature of these flavonoids supported their use for human radiation protection. Both compounds provided protection against death from gastrointestinal syndrome, as well as Bone Marrow Syndrome, and the researchers suggested that the radioprotection of the flavonoids might be due to their free radical scavenging antioxidant activity (Devi *et al.*, 1998; Uma Devi *et al.*, 1999).

Antioxidant activity

Balanehru and Nagarajan (1991) found that ursolic acid from *Ocimum sanctum* offered 60% protection against free radical-induced damage in rat liver microsomes. Tulsi did not induce lipid peroxidation, which further supports its therapeutic application in humans. The researchers also studied the free radical scavenging potential of ursolic acid in the cardiac lipid membrane peroxidation and found protection of heart and liver microsomes (Balanehru and Nagarajan, 1992). In budding and early flowering stages, *Ocimum* oils are rich in monoterpenes (Lemberkovics *et al.*, 1998). Panda and Kar (1998) studied antioxidant activity of Tulsi extract (0.5gm/kg) over 15 days and found a decrease in T4, hepatic lipid peroxidation (LPO), glucose-6-phosphatase (G-6-P) activity. Activities of endogenous antioxidant enzyme superoxide dismutase (SOD) and catalase (CAT) were increased by the extract.

Central nervous system effect

An ethanol extract of the leaves of Tulsi was screened for its effects on the central nervous system. Tulsi prolonged the time of lost reflex in mice due to pentobarbital, decreased the recovery time and severity of electroshock and pentylenetetrazole-induced convulsions, and decreased apomorphine-induced fighting time and ambulation in "open field" studies. Using a behavioral despair model involving forced swimming in rats and mice, the extract lowered immobility in a manner comparable to imipramine. This action was blocked by haloperidol and sulpiride, indicating a possible action involving dopaminergic neurons. In similar studies, there was a synergistic action when the extract was combined with bromocriptine, a potent D2-receptor agonist. (Sakina *et al.*, 1990)

Noise stress audiogenic seizure-induced increase in plasma corticosterone level in rats was prevented by ethanol extract of Tulsi, (Sembulingam *et al.*, 1997). Tulsi has a very mild tranquilizing effect on mice without significant changes in body temperature and behavior (Krishnamurthy, 1959; Singh *et al.*, 1970).

Immunomodulatory effect

A methanol extract and an aqueous suspension of *Ocimum sanctum* leaves were investigated for their immunoregulatory profile in response to antigenic challenge of *Salmonella typhosa* and sheep erythrocytes in albino rats. The study demonstrated an immunostimulation of humoral immunologic response as represented by an increase in antibody titre in both the Widal and sheep erythrocyte agglutination tests, as well as by the cellular immune response represented by E-rosette formation and lymphocytosis (Godhwani *et al.*, 1988). Essential oils of leaves of *Ocimum sanctum* and fixed oil of Tulsi seeds were investigated for some humoral and cell-mediated immune responses in non-stressed and stressed animals. In non-stressed subjects, both substances produced significant increase in the anti-sheep red blood cells (SRBC) antibody titre, a measure of humoral immune response, and decrease in footpad thickness and percent leucocyte migration inhibition measures of cell-mediated immune response[F28] (Mediratta *et al.*, 1987 and Mediratta and Sharma, 2000). Recently in 2002 Mediratta *et. al.*, reported Tulsi's immuno-modulatory effects to be mediated by GABAergic pathways. Vana Tulsi (*Ocimum gratissimum*) was found to improve phagocytic function without affecting humoral or cell-mediated immune system (Atal *et al.*, 1996). The immunosuppressant effect of restraint stress on humoral and cell-mediated immune responses was effectively blocked by pretreating the animals with Tulsi leaf oil as well as seed oil (Mediratta and Sharma, 2000).

[F28] Humoral immune response of the body: response of the immune system to antigens through B-cell lymphocytes; they produce free antibodies which circulate in the blood stream and destroy the antigens.

Anti-AIDS effect

The water-soluble polar substances from *Ocimum basilicum* (a close basil relative of Tulsi) showed potent anti-HIV-1 activity induced cytopathogenecity in MT-4 cells. In addition, these aqueous extracts inhibited giant cell formation in co-culture of Molt-4 cells with and without HIV-1 infection and showed inhibitory activity against HIV-1 reverse transcription (Yamasaki *et al.,* 1998).

Anti-insect activity, malaria and encephalitis

Tulsi extracts have been shown to have insecticidal activity (e.g., killing mosquito, ticks and their larvae) (Chopra *et al.,* 1941; Deshpande and Tipnis, 1977; Sharma and Wattal, 1979; Chavan and Nikam, 1982; Kelm and Nair, 1998). Tulsi also has significant insect repellent effects. In 1904, Sir George Wordwood published a report of Tulsi's mosquito repellent activity in The Times (published in Bombay), and later experimental studies have confirmed this property (Roy *et al.,* 1976; Vaidya, 1985). The English called Tulsi the "mosquito plant", as it was found that wherever Tulsi is grown, fewer mosquitoes are seen. Tulsi's direct therapeutic effect in the treatment and prevention of malaria was reported in ancient Ayurvedic literature and confirmed in modern times (Roy *et al.,* 1976).

Antibacterial and antitubercular activity

The essential oils of *Ocimum sanctum* Tulsi possess *in vivo* and *in vitro* antibacterial activity against staphylococci and other bacteria (Bhat and Broker, 1955; Khurana and Vagikar, 1959; Narasimha Rao and Nigam, 1970; Grover and Rao, 1977; Sawhney *et al.,* 1977; Suri and Thind, 1978; Mehta *et al.,* 1978-79; Lahariya

and Rao, 1979; Singh and Pathak, 1979; Patel and Bhatt, 1988). Tulsi is useful in the treatment of abscesses and other localized infections. Bataru *et al.,* (1999) discovered antibacterial activity in *Ocimum gratissimum* as well. Tulsi has antitubercular activity (Gupta and Vishwanathan, 1955; Ramaswami and Sirsi, 1967).

Antiviral activity

Tefroli an Ayurvedic preparation containing Tulsi has been found to be effective against viral hepatitis. An antiviral effect of dry powder of Tulsi leaves has been demonstrated in chicken infected with IBD virus (Kolte *et al.,* 1999). The antiviral activity of the juice of Tulsi leaves has been well documented for the top-necrosis virus of the pea plant (Roy *et al.,* 1979) and other plant viruses (Singh, 1972; Tripathi and Tripathi, 1982).

Cholesterol effects

A mild cholesterol-lowering effect of Tulsi was observed by Pushpangadan and Sobti, (1977). Saponins, components of Tulsi, have the capacity of forming stable complexes with cholesterol and other 3-beta-hydroxy steroids (precursors of cholesterol), thereby exhibiting *hypocholesterolemic properties* (Sirtori *et al.,* 1979). Restraint-induced stress increase in cholesterol was lowered by Tulsi and its constituent eugenol (Sen *et al.,* 1992). Administration of fresh leaves of Tulsi mixed as 1gm and 2gm in 100gms of diet given to normal albino rabbits for four weeks, brought about significant lowering in serum total cholesterol, triglycerides, phospholipid and low density lipoproteins (LDL) ("bad cholesterol") levels and significant increase in the high-density lipoproteins (HDL) ("good cholesterol") and total fecal sterol contents (Sarkar *et al.,* 1994).

Cardiovascular effects

Studies carried out on dogs, rabbits and other animals show a *hypotensive* (blood pressure lowering) action, brought about by peripheral, vascular dilatation and by a direct cardiac effect. There is also a transient, stimulant effect on respiration, possibly due to a blood pressure lowering effect (Krishnamurthy, 1959; Singh *et al.*, 1970). Some anticoagulase factors are present in Tulsi, which may be responsible for its mild anticoagulant, antithrombotic effect (Bhat and Broker, 1954).

Anticancer activity

In a Japanese study, edible Japanese plants were screened for nitric oxide generation inhibitory activities. Methanolic extract of *Ocimum* varieties markedly inhibited nitric oxide synthase activity. The results suggest that basil and various other edible plants contain secondary metabolites with cancer preventive activity through reduction of excess amounts of nitric oxide (Kim *et al.*, 1998).

Tulsi significantly decreases the incidence of benzo(a)pyrene- induced neoplasia (squamous cell carcinoma in stomach of mice) and 3-methyldimethylaminoazobenzene induced hepatomas in rats (Aruna and Sivaramakrishnan, 1992). Topical treatment with the ethanolic Tulsi leaf extract produced significant reduction in the values of tumor incidence (papillomas) in the skin of albino mice (Prashar *et al.*, 1994). Tulsi leaves have also been shown to induce carcinogen detoxifying enzyme glutathione-S-tranferase (GST) in Swiss mice (Aruna and Sivaramakrishnan, 1990). The component terpene ùrosolic acid has been demonstrated to have anticancer activity (Rastogi and Mehrotra, 1995a).

Tulsi, in the form of fresh leaf paste, aqueous extract and ethanolic extract were topically applied and the extracts were orally administered to buccal pouch mucosa of animals exposed to 0.5% of dimethylbenz (a) anthracene. Incidence of papillomas and squamous cell carcinomas were significantly reduced, and there was increased survival rate with the topically applied leaf paste and orally administered extracts. The orally administered aqueous extract showed greater effect than fresh leaf paste and ethanolic extract (Karthikeyan *et al.*, 1999).

Intestinal effects

Ocimum gratissimum was found to possess antidiarrheal activity against several bacteria and was most effective against *Shigella dysenterae* (Omoregbe *et al.*, 1996). Extracts of *Ocimum sanctum* have been shown to have antidiarrheal effect in rats (Godhwani *et al.*, 1987; Offiah and Chikwendu, 1999). A direct smooth muscle relaxant activity on the rabbit ileum is described (Kashinathan *et al.*, 1972). Tulsi oil, and eugenol extracted from it, have marked relaxant effect on the trachea and lesser relaxant effect on ileal muscles (Reiter and Brandt, 1985).

Anti-inflammatory activity

Aqueous and methanolic extract of Tulsi inhibited acute and chronic inflammation in rats (Godhwani *et al.*, 1987). In another study *Ocimum sanctum* fixed oil showed potent anti-inflammatory activity in rats, due primarily to its linolenic oil content (Singh and Majumdar, 1997, 1999). Singh *et al.*, (1996) reported anti-inflammatory activity in Tulsi fixed oil possibly due to its fatty acids. Singh, (1998) has further reported that not only *Ocimum sanctum* but other *Ocimum* species, such as *Ocimum basilicum* and *Ocimum americanum* also have anti-inflammatory activities. This is likely due to the presence of linolenic acid in these species. Tulsi contains other phytonutrients (e.g., ursolic acid and oleanolic acid) that have significant cyclo-oxygenase-2 (COX-2) inhibitory effect. COX-2 inflammation is thought to lie at the root of many diseases, including cancer, Alzheimer's disease and many forms of arthritis (Newmark and Schulick, 2000).

Antiulcer activity

The fixed oil of Tulsi was found to possess significant antiulcer activity against aspirin, indomethacin, alcohol, histamine, reserpine, serotonin and stress-induced ulceration in experimental animals. Significant inhibition was also observed in gastric secretion and aspirin-induced gastric ulceration in pylorus ligated rats (Mandal *et al.*, 1993). The lipoxygenase inhibitory, histamine antagonistic and antisecretory effects of the oil probably contributed to the antiulcer activity (Singh and Majumdar, 1999).

Fertility and reproductive issues

Some group of researchers have reported a decrease in sexual activity and antifertile effects in both female and male mice and rats with large doses of Tulsi and various extracts. There are also reports of implantation problems in female rats, and inconsistent findings of embryo toxicity with high doses. (Chopra, *et al.*, 1956; Vohara *et al.*, 1968, 1969; Batta and Santhakumari, 1971; Kashinathan *et al.*, 1972; Seth, *et al.*, 1981; Khanna *et al.*, 1986). In discussing their research, Kashinathan *et al.*, (1972) state, "It appears that the sterility is due to intake of high amounts of Tulsi leaves... Some toxicity may also arise from the very high doses of Tulsi used– e.g., 465mg/day/mouse for 30 to 90 days, which correspond to very large doses in man."

Such reports of reproduction problems in rodents are in direct contrast to the many classic Ayurvedic references to Tulsi's profertile effects in humans noted earlier, as well as our own clinical experience (e.g., see Case Study # 4 in *Appendix A*). This raises important questions regarding the validity of the rodent model in predicting reproductive effects in humans, as well as issues of dose, dosage form and mode of administration. Clarifying these issues may be given higher research priority. This topic is discussed further in Chapter 7.

Other effects

Anabolic activity

Growth-promoting anabolic activity of Tulsi leaves was found in animals (Malviya and Gupta, 1971).

Antipyretic (fever lowering) activity

Aqueous and methanolic extracts of Tulsi have fever lowering effect in rats (Godhwani *et al.*, 1987).

Antiasthmatic activity

Components of Tulsi (myrcenol and nerol) have been demonstated to have antiasthmatic activity (Rastogi and Mehrotra, 1995b).

Liver protection

The hepatoprotective effect of Tulsi has been further documented by Seethalakshmi *et al.*, 1982.

Antifilarial worm activity

Tulsi leaf extract inhibits the enzymes of filarial worm *Setaria digitata* in cattle (Banu *et al.*, 1992).

Antifungal activity

The essential oils of *Ocimum sanctum* and *Ocimum gratissimum* have strong antifungal properties (Kaul and Nigam, 1977; Narasimha Rao and Subba Rao, 1972; Suri and Thind, 1979a, 1979b; Singh *et al.,* 1980; Nwosu and Okafor, 1995).

Thyroid activity

Panda and Kar (1998) found that *Ocimum sanctum* leaf extract significantly decreased serum thyroxine (T4) concentration. However, there were no marked changes in triiodothyronine (T3) level or in T3/T4 ratio. Such activity may be helpful in treating hyperthyroidism.

Human clinical studies

Antiviral activity

Tulsi is used as an effective medicine against viral hepatitis (Sankaran, 1980). Extracts of leaves of *Ocimum sanctum* showed highly significant clinical and biochemical clearance of viral hepatitis (Rajalakshmi *et al.,* 1988; Rastogi and Mehrotra, 1995a).

Pulmonary and bronchial antioxidant benefits

Siurin (1997) studied the effects of herbal essential oils (including *Ocimum*) on peroxidation-antioxidant defense and lipid metabolism in 150 patients with bronchitis. Lowering of plasma levels of dienic conjugates and ketones, and activation of catalase in red cells characteristic of antioxidant effect were observed. Tulsi has been shown to be effective in treating tropical pulmonary eosinophilia caused by parasitic worm infection (Sivarajan and Balachandran, 1994).

Anti-inflammatory and antiarthritic activity

Several researchers have found Tulsi to be effective in reducing the inflammatory conditions of joints and in relieving suffering in arthritis (Anonymous, 1966; Lim-Sylianco *et al.*, 1985; Lasker, 1981).

Antidiabetic activity

Tulsi has been shown to be effective in non-insulin dependent diabetes mellitius (type 2) (Agarwal *et al.,* 1995). A significant decline in blood and urine glucose level was shown with Tulsi as compared to a control group (Pushpangadan and Sobti, 1977). The effects of Tulsi on fasting and after–meal blood glucose and serum cholesterol levels were studied in humans. Tulsi decreased both fasting and after meal blood glucose levels significantly (Agarwal *et al.,* 1996).

Antiulcer activity

Tulsi has shown to be useful in the prevention and treatment of stress-related gastric ulcers (Jalil, 1970).

Postoperative peritoneal adhesion

Tulsi is effective in preventing postoperative peritoneal adhesion after abdominal surgery (Shenoy, 1998).

Cardiovascular protection

Tulsi has been shown to have a cardiovascular– friendly effect in patients of coronary artery diseases (Dwivedi *et al.*, 2000).

Periodontal health

Fresh Tulsi leaf extract showed protection against human plaque cultures and gram-negative oral bacterias, and was corrective in severely infected cases (Bhandari, 1970a, 1970b; Patel and Bhatt, 1988).

7

Summary, Discussion and Conclusions

This book presents a historical, cultural and scientific introduction to Ayurveda and India's sacred basil Tulsi. The health promoting and medicinal properties of Tulsi are documented here through classical Ayurvedic references and corroborating experimental and clinical studies. For the sake of brevity and ease of reading, topic references that have been noted previously in the text are generally not repeated in this summary.

History

The Indian sacred herb Tulsi (or Tulasi) has been known for its medicinal value for thousands of years. The earliest known account of Ayurvedic knowledge was written about 7000 years ago in the *Rigveda*, which states that herbs, by their healing properties, give happiness and peace of mind. Ayurveda is the "Science of Life" of Hinduism, which is not simply a religion but a way of life by which humans can coexist skillfully with nature. Ayurveda represents a holistic approach to health and well-being. The importance of herbs for maintaining vitality, preventing disease, restoring health and prolonging life is documented in various ancient Ayurvedic textbooks (2700BC to 1200AD) in which Tulsi is described as a main pillar of herbal medicine. Among the many medicinal herbs of India, it holds the supreme position as the "Mother Medicine of Nature" in these texts. For medicinal use, three types of Tulsi are of primary interest: two varieties of *Ocimum sanctum* (Krishna and Rama Tulsi) and one wild variety, *Ocimum gratissimum* (Vana Tulsi). The highly esteemed selection of the Tulsi plant by Indians over the millennia is one of the examples where humans have chosen and cultivated the plants that are most favorable and beneficial to them.

Seen as a goddess incarnated in plant form, Tulsi has been included by the ancient rishis (the sages and healers of those times) in the worship of the deities, and was made part of the prasad (an offering by the devotee to the deity, given back by the priests to the devotee). This charanamrita is an example of the socialization of medical knowledge through religious ritual. In this way, people at all levels of society consumed Tulsi leaves frequently to their great benefit. In addition to their extensive practical experience, ancient rishis must have had an intuitive knowledge of the properties of Tulsi, which balances altered physiological functions of the body and allows humans to adapt better in circumstances of health and disease, living a healthier, better and longer life. As a sacred plant, Tulsi is worshipped and venerated daily by traditional Hindus, and is part of all such households today.

Ayurveda and antistress/ adaptogenic concepts

The range of Tulsi's medicinal properties is remarkably vast. It is recommended for treating a great many different disorders and is widely taken daily for promoting general health and preventing disease. Reading the ancient texts made us aware that this unusually diverse range of medicinal activity is likely largely the results of what we now call the *adaptogenic/antistress property* of Tulsi. An adaptogen/antistress agent is one that helps the body to generally cope with stress and to return to a normal healthy state when disturbed. Tulsi is the most effective known adaptogen.

In Ayurveda, the term *tridosha* means the three disharmonies in the body. In our interpretation, the first, vata is related to energy formation and conservation, tissue respiration and related mechanisms. The second, pitta is related to the enzymes and neurohumoral (neurological systems and their related hormones) systems in the body. The third, kapha is related to water and electrolyte balance. A predominance of one dosha, suppressing the others, results in a disease

related to that particular system of the body.

Tulsi contains multiple bioactive substances, including minerals and vitamins, that normalize the disturbed physiological functions of the body by harmonizing the different imbalances (energy formation/ conservation and tissue respiration, neurological system and neurohormones, and water electrolyte system). This regulating faculty of Tulsi is consistent with the ancient Ayurvedic concept of tridosha balance and with our modern antistress/adaptogenic concept.

The rapid advancement of modern civilization, with its industrialization and over population, has brought about an increase in stressors of diverse nature, including over-crowding, atmospheric pollution, poor nutrition and food adulteration, fast, over-ambitious and competitive lifestyle, physical inactivity, noise, wars and related fears, family isolation and many synthetic drugs. As an ever–adapting organism, we have been able to withstand these stressful stimuli to a great extent, but the continued negative effects of excessive stress (distress) manifest themselves in many serious degenerative stress diseases depending on the genetic weakness of the individual. The weaker link of the chain breaks when it is stretched irrespective of the direction in which it is pulled — viz. a chronic tooth sepsis (persistent stress) may result in diabetes in one individual and hypertension in the other, depending on the predisposed genetic susceptibility. Recently, stress has been implicated in the genesis of variety of diseases, including general atherosclerosis, coronary and cerebral sclerosis, premature aging, chronic liver, kidney and bronchial diseases, malignomas, migraine, psychopathology, hypertension, diabetes mellitus, arthritis,

Tulsi's role in the prevention and treatment of stress disorders

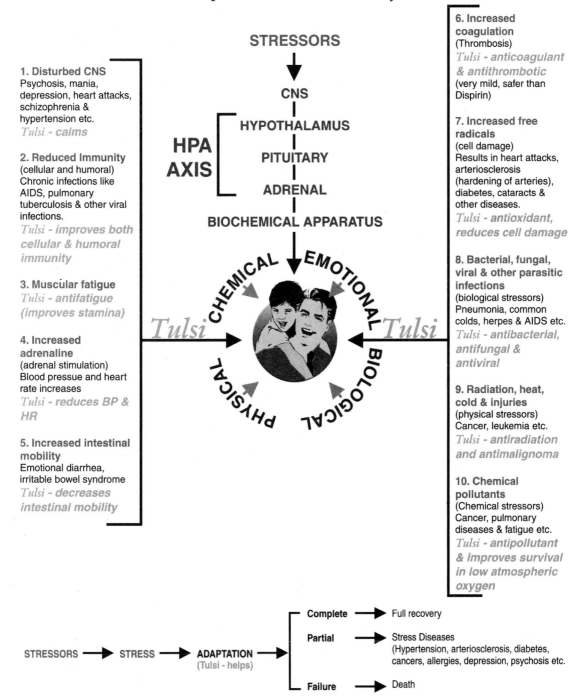

6. Increased coagulation
(Thrombosis)
Tulsi - anticoagulant & antithrombotic
(very mild, safer than Dispirin)

7. Increased free radicals
(cell damage)
Results in heart attacks, arteriosclerosis (hardening of arteries), diabetes, cataracts & other diseases.
Tulsi - antioxidant, reduces cell damage

8. Bacterial, fungal, viral & other parasitic infections
(biological stressors)
Pneumonia, common colds, herpes & AIDS etc.
Tulsi - antibacterial, antifungal & antiviral

9. Radiation, heat, cold & injuries
(physical stressors)
Cancer, leukemia etc.
Tulsi - antiradiation and antimalignoma

10. Chemical pollutants
(Chemical stressors)
Cancer, pulmonary diseases & fatigue etc.
Tulsi - antipollutant & improves survival in low atmospheric oxygen

1. Disturbed CNS
Psychosis, mania, depression, heart attacks, schizophrenia & hypertension etc.
Tulsi - calms

2. Reduced Immunity
(cellular and humoral)
Chronic infections like AIDS, pulmonary tuberculosis & other viral infections.
Tulsi - improves both cellular & humoral immunity

3. Muscular fatigue
Tulsi - antifatigue (improves stamina)

4. Increased adrenaline
(adrenal stimulation)
Blood pressue and heart rate increases
Tulsi - reduces BP & HR

5. Increased intestinal mobility
Emotional diarrhea, irritable bowel syndrome
Tulsi - decreases intestinal mobility

STRESSORS
CNS
HYPOTHALAMUS
PITUITARY
ADRENAL
HPA AXIS
BIOCHEMICAL APPARATUS

CHEMICAL — EMOTIONAL — PHYSICAL — BIOLOGICAL

Tulsi

STRESSORS → STRESS → **ADAPTATION** *(Tulsi - helps)* →

Complete → Full recovery
Partial → Stress Diseases (Hypertension, arteriosclerosis, diabetes, cancers, allergies, depression, psychosis etc.
Failure → Death

Fig 14 : As shown in this figure, Tulsi calms the mind, improves both cellular and humoral immunity, enhances stamina and reduces fatigue, lowers high blood pressure and increased heart rate due to stress, decreases stress-induced intestinal motility, reduces increased coagulation (thrombosis) occurring during stress, and protects against radiation, free radical damage, pollution, and bacterial, viral and fungal infections, malignomas and improves oxygen utilization.

cancer and other degenerative disorders.

The failure of body mechanisms to effectively cope with the adverse effects of stress results in stress-induced diseases. Any drug that can stimulate (buck-up) the failing mechanisms and thus antagonize or prevent the negative effects of stress, can be called an *antistress* drug. Modern medicine has some agents, like the tranquillizer diazepam, which allay anxiety and prevent some effects of stress where mental tension is the main cause. However, strictly speaking, these are not true antistress/adaptogenic drug, as they reduce physical activity and endurance and depress the sensorium with general sedative activity.

Figure 14 depicts possible effects in human biological systems induced by various physical, chemical, biological and psychological/emotional stressors and shows how Tulsi affects these changes as an adaptogen/antistress agent.

The antistress property of Tulsi and other plants reveals a novel class of drugs that should set new trends in prevention and therapy of stress diseases. The research work of our group and other scientists in this field supports our contention that Tulsi is a very safe and effective adaptogen for long-term prevention and treatment of all kinds of stress-induced ill effects on human body systems.

Tulsi effects

Stress endurance and antifatigue effect

We have conducted experimental studies on animals and human clinical trials to demonstrate Tulsi's antistress/adaptogenic and endurance-enhancing properties through standard modern scientific techniques.

In animals, Tulsi improves physical performance and endurance under physical stress such as forced swimming. This is called a *staminator effect* (i.e., increases stamina). Tulsi was found to prevent restraint ulcers (immobilization-induced ulcers), cold-stress ulcers and chemical (acetylsalicylic acid) stress-induced ulcers in rats. Tulsi reduces the typical stress-induced changes in the function of the adrenal glands. The adrenal glands are like batteries in the body and are often drained with periods of prolonged stress and strenuous activity. Tulsi protects and "fuels" the adrenal glands. Apart from its action on these glands, Tulsi also has another, non-adrenal beneficial effect, by which it acts through SDH (succinate dehydrogenase) and other neurotransmitters. This has been shown through Tulsi's antistress effects and increasing swimming performance, even on animals from which the adrenal glands have been removed. We compared Tulsi to synthetic drugs such as corticosteroids, stimulants, tranquilizers and sedatives. The tranquillizers and sedatives have an antianxiety effect in humans, but do not improve physical performance and often decrease it. The stimulants and corticosteroids directly enhance short-term physical performance in athletes, but cannot be used to improve endurance in the long run because of their serious side effects such as muscle necrosis. In contrast, Tulsi significantly increases endurance and physical performance, as well as the ability to cope with stress without negative side effects.

In human clinical studies, Tulsi has been shown to reduce fatigue. This capacity of Tulsi makes it an ideal treatment for chronic fatigue syndrome and for aging patients, who often complain about increasing fatigue. Furthermore, fatigue is often a key factor in various types of vehicular and industrial accidents (e.g., Adam, 1997). Daily use of Tulsi may well play a preventive role in reducing fatigue and fatigue-related accidents.

Adaptive biochemical effects during stress

The enzyme *succinate dehydrogenase* (SDH) assists the formation and conservation of energy–forming systems in the body's cells. Tulsi has shown to help the formation of this enzyme in the brains of rats. Research suggests that Tulsi may also assist the formation of SDH in the human brain. This may be one of the major mechanisms responsible for Tulsi's antistress and staminator activities.

The ability of Tulsi to decrease the neurotransmitter *5-hydroxytryptamine* (5-HT or serotonin) in the brain during prolonged severe stress is also likely of considerable importance. In cases of schizophrenia, 5-HT may play an important role in the genesis of this disease; Tulsi may be useful in the management of the disease.

Central nervous system effects

Tulsi shows a mild tranquilizing effect, reduces aggressive behavior under stress and increases tolerance to noise in rats. Tulsi prevents the increased plasma cortico-sterone level induced by audiogenic seizures (noise-stress) and also showed antidepressant activity in animals. Tulsi can be useful in helping people to cope with the noisy environment of city life, as it has a calming and antidepressant effect on the psyche.

Comparison of Tulsi with other adaptogens

In 1969, Brekhman and Dardymov described some plants, such as *Eleutherococcus senticosus* (Siberian ginseng) and *Panax ginseng* (Chinese ginseng), which help the individual to cope better with stress. We compared Tulsi with these two well-known adaptogens, and found Tulsi to be most potent as well as the least toxic. The safety margin was much higher for Tulsi than the two forms of ginseng; the toxicity of Tulsi is negligible in the doses recommended in the prevention and treatment of disease. This finding has become increasingly important with the growing use of *Panax ginseng* as a tonic/medicine especially since that herb has been reported to produce a corticoid-like syndrome with insomnia, edema, hypertension and withdrawal symptoms (restlessness and diarrhea) with high dose use.

Antioxidant protection against free radical damage

Exposure to chemical or industrial toxins, air pollution, tobacco, smoke, alcohol, ultraviolet radiation, X-rays, TV, computers, mental stress, excess heat and burns as well as other factors, puts the human body in danger of undesirable *free radicals*[F29]. Animal studies have shown that Tulsi has a protective effect against free radical damage (lipid peroxidation) in normal cells and their membranes. We presume that this property can be extended

---

[F29] Although essential for higher beings, oxygen has the potential for metabolic toxicity. Free radicals are unstable molecules that react with other molecules to acquire reactive oxygen, setting off a chain reaction. An excess of free radicals can cause different medical conditions, depending on which tissues are attacked. In normal cellular metabolism, free radicals get formed from moment to moment. These free radicals have, amongst other properties, an enormous affinity to react with cell membranes and to damage their integrity through lipid peroxidation. If the body is in a healthy state the destruction and formation of cells is balanced, but during aging and pathological conditions, the formation of free radicals markedly increases and cell destruction tends to dominate

to humans. Usually, the antioxidants that are effective in animals are also effective in humans – e.g., the antioxidant properties of vitamin E have been well demonstrated in many species.

The antioxidant free radical scavenging capacity of Tulsi may protect sensitive structures such as cellular membranes, lipoproteins, DNA, wall of arterial blood vessels and enzymes from undesired oxidation. Free radical damage and lipid peroxidation increases with age. Tulsi may play a key role in the prevention of heart disease and other free radical damage-related diseases such as cancer, as well as premature aging – some of the main concerns of our modern civilization. Tulsi is rich in carotene, vitamin C (ascorbic acid), selenium and essential oils, which are well known for their antioxidant activity. Tulsi provides its antioxidant effect in the form of a herb which is an advantage because the absorption of plant nutrients is generally much easier than that of synthetic antioxidants.

Immunomodulatory effects

Tulsi enhances the cell-mediated immune response in humans, as well as animals. Treatment with Tulsi increases the number of the T-lymphocytes, the white blood cells responsible for immune defense. The cell-mediated immune response is reduced in immune deficiency diseases, including AIDS and cancer, as well as in normal aging. Aqueous extract of Tulsi showed inhibitory effect against HIV-1 reverse transcription. A direct anticancer activity has been shown using Tulsi's terpene component ursolic acid, as well with other terpene. Tulsi can be useful as a supplementary or complementary treatment along with other therapies in cancer and other immune system compromised diseases to

improve the ability of the individual to fight these disorders.

The current opinion estimates that between two and ten years typically pass after infection before the full symptoms of AIDS appear. Patients who are HIV positive and who don't suffer yet from AIDS-related diseases may benefit from a long-term treatment with Tulsi, which may prevent the onset of the disease through T-lymphocyte increase and other mechanisms. The results of our studies on the immunomodulator and antistress activities of Tulsi are strong pointers for its effectiveness in AIDS. Tulsi, in its capacity as an antioxidant and an antistress agent, may improve the stamina and survival time of patients receiving modern allopathic treatment, as well as those not receiving any other treatment. Note that the medicinal effect of Tulsi should be observed over months, as often only a prolonged use has the desired medicinal effect.

Antiaging effect

The phenomenon of aging is very complex and much research has been done in the last few decades with the goal of understanding and slowing down the process of aging, especially premature aging. Aging manifests as a decrease in adaptive capacity. It is possible to help the optimal functioning of the self-regulatory and adaptive processes of the cells and thus slow down the advance of aging (Petkov, 1975). We have conducted many studies on Indian Ayurvedic plants since 1976, and found evidence that it is possible to retard the aging process with adaptogenic/antistress herbs. We definitely know that stress, free radicals and reduced immunity have a major role in the aging process, and that Tulsi is effective in reducing the negative impact of these factors.

It has been shown that free radical damage and particularly lipid peroxidation of the cell membranes increase with age. Amongst other adverse effect, free radicals induce a gradual decline of endocrine glands and their hormones, as well as a resistance of the cells to the effect of these hormones. Tulsi normalizes the function and hormone level of the adrenals, increases the sensitivity of the nervous system to the adrenal hormones and slows down aging.

The T-lymphocytes are the white blood cells responsible for immune defense of the body, and the T-cell-mediated immune response is reduced in aging. Tulsi has the capacity to reduce the negative impact of aging by increasing the number of T-lymphocytes and improving, likewise, the body's immunity.

Pulmonary and bronchial benefits

In animal studies, Tulsi has been shown to reduce bronchospasm (spasm of airways/the wall of the bronchi and bronchioles) and associated mortality. In human clinical studies, Tulsi was found to be effective in bronchial asthma, improving considerably the pulmonary function of the patients (Singh *et al.,* 1986). These patients experienced fewer asthmatic attacks, increased expectoration, reduction of breathlessness, and a slower rate of respiration, as well as an overall feeling of improvement. The measurement of the objective parameters of pulmonary function showed a free respiratory act (bronchodilator effect) increased pulmonary volume and better capacity to exhale forcibly and remove dyspnea. These changes were accompanied by an increase in hemoglobin and body weight. The expectorant and bronchodilator effect of Tulsi started from the first day of treatment and reached its maximum after one month of treatment. Two components of Tulsi, myrcenol and nerol, have been separately shown to have antiasthmatic activity in humans and are likely to be responsible for the major antiasthmatic effect of the plant.

Allergic reactions play an important role in the genesis of bronchial asthma. Tulsi's antiallergic effect is detectable in the decrease of eosinophil leukocytes[F30] in blood and sputum of asthma patients. An increasing number of allergens, such as pollen, chemicals and other pollutants, are affecting our lives and increasing allergy related diseases. The antiallergic property of Tulsi has been shown to be useful in cases of tropical pulmonary eosinophilia, a disorder which shows asthmatic symptoms connected to very high counts of eosinophil leukocytes in the blood. The regular use of Tulsi may have a protective effect against allergic diseases.

In Ayurveda and folklore medicine Tulsi has been used as a treatment for nasal inflammation (coryza) and bronchitis since time immemorial, and forms the central ingredient of many household remedies for these common disorders.

In experimental and clinical studies, Tulsi has been shown to inhibit the growth of tubercular bacilli. The effect is not very marked, but in combination with modern antitubercular drugs this property of Tulsi, along with its antistress effects, can be very useful in patients with tuberculosis.

Arterial hypertension reduction

In animal studies, Tulsi showed a transient, hypotensive effect, possibly due to vascular dilatation and mild cardiac-depression. In a

---

[F30] The eosinophil leukocytes reflect amongst other reasons the reaction of the body against allergies.

placebo-controlled clinical study, Tulsi significantly reduced mild forms of arterial hypertension, especially when the rise in blood pressure was idiopathic and likely stress-related. Tulsi can be used for prevention and long-term treatment of arterial hypertension, as it reduces the blood pressure smoothly to acceptable levels and is free from side effects, an important advantage compared to synthetic cardiovascular drugs, all of which create serious adverse side effects. Tulsi leaf, taken for at least a month, can act as a preventive measure for persons prone to hypertension who show a casual moderate hypertension. This initial unstable stage usually converts into established hypertension after some time; this progression may be avoided with Tulsi.

Improved tolerance to anoxia

In animals, Tulsi has been found to increase the tolerance to lack of oxygen and help survival in air with low oxygen concentration. This is likely a very important property for humans given today's atmospheric pollution and decreasing oxygen content–especially in modern urban settings.

Prevention and treatment of gastric ulcers

The stressful and competitive modern lifestyle can induce gastric ulcers. Tulsi has been shown to protect against chemical and stress-induced gastric ulcers in animal experiments and has been demonstrated to be useful in prevention and treatment of gastric ulcers in human clinical studies. It appears the Tulsi works against gastric ulcers primarily by reducing the effect of stress, although Tulsi's antibacterial properties may also be relevant in some cases.

Liver protection

Tulsi has been known for thousands of years as a treatment for jaundice, including what is now known as viral hepatitis. Modern science has confirmed theses benefits. Diabetes mellitus, hepatitis, cardiovascular and pulmonary diseases, parasites and other diseases as well as poor nutrition, certain modern drug, alcohol and other toxic agents that are common in modern society, can reduce liver function and produce disease. Long-term use of Tulsi may protect the liver against such disorders.

Encephalitis benefits

Tulsi is effective against Japanese viral encephalitis Type B. Patients treated with Tulsi had a higher survival rate than patients treated with the standard therapy of steroids and showed a very low incidence of neurological defects after recovery from encephalitis. Viral encephalitis usually causes significant nervous system defects.

Intestinal motility and antidiarrheal effects

Tulsi reduces the intestinal peristalsis and slows down the passage of food through the intestines in animals. Tulsi also has antidiarrheal activity against several bacteria. This suggests the use of Tulsi in patients with hypermotile intestines as a long-term treatment.

Diabetes mellitus benefits

In animal and human clinical studies, Tulsi has been shown to be effective in coping with diabetes mellitus. In forms of non-insulin dependent diabetes mellitus, Tulsi significantly decreases blood and urine glucose levels. It can be used as a supplement to allopathic medicine in diabetes mellitus and in cases of slightly increased blood sugar level, it might be the medicine of first choice. Tulsi may also reduce the insulin resistance in some cases of diabetes mellitus.

Cholesterol effects

Tulsi produces a mild cholesterol lowering effect in humans (Singh *et al.*, 1998 and Steinberg, 1993) and animals. Administration of fresh Tulsi leaves in the diet for four weeks, brought about significant changes in the lipid profile of normal albino rabbits. This resulted in significant lowering in serum total cholesterol, triglyceride, phospholipid and low-density lipoprotein (LDL)-cholesterol levels, and significant increase in the high-density lipoproteins (HDL)-cholesterol (which is considered beneficial) and total fecal sterol contents. Saponin components of Tulsi have the capacity to lower cholesterol through formation of stable complexes with cholesterol and 3-beta-hydroxy steroids (precursors of cholesterol). Stress-induced increase in cholesterol was lowered by Tulsi and its component eugenol. Since oxidative stress is an additional mechanism of arteriosclerosis, one that might take place alongside hyperlipidemia, it is possible that agents like Tulsi, with hypolipidemic and antioxidant effects be preferred in the management of arteriosclerosis. The current opinion is that oxidatively modified LDL (low-density lipoprotein) cholesterol is cytotoxic and damages endothelial cells. Increased numbers of these damaged cells are found in patients with coronary heart disease.

Anticoagulant and antithrombotic effects

The cardiovascular friendly effect of Tulsi has been demonstrated in patients with coronary artery diseases. Tulsi has mild anticoagulant action which may be useful for patients with atherosclerosis (such as coronary heart disease or cerebral atherosclerosis), who are normally treated with low doses of aspirin for platelet aggregation inhibition. Some patients cannot use aspirin because of risks of hemorrhagic side effects. Also in some cases the indication for therapy with strong allopathic thrombocyte aggregation inhibitors is doubtful. Tulsi can be a milder, alternative antithrombotic medicine, an ideal agent for long-term treatment and prevention of blood clots in all arterial blood vessels of the body. In this regard Tulsi use would likely be helpful in decreasing the recently reported incidence of blood clots forming in the limbs of passengers during prolong intercontinental air plain travel.

Antiradiation effect

In animal studies, a potent antiradiation effect of Tulsi has been shown with a very significant reduction of radiation-induced damage and mortality. This finding is particularly relevant to persons exposed to excess radiation, such as those:

- working with radiodiagnosis and therapy (e.g., nuclear medicine, angiography, operations under X-ray control)
- receiving radiotherapy for malignoma
- working in atomic reactors and other units with exposure to radiation
- regularly exposed to high altitude solar radiation (e.g., airline personnel)
- chronically exposed to TV and computer screens

Anti-inflammatory and antipyretic (antifever) effects

In Ayurvedic textbooks, Tulsi's ability to reduce fever and inflammation is widely described. These beneficial effects on inflammation and fever have also been verified in animal and human clinical studies.

Rheumatoid arthritis treatment

When Tulsi was given to patients with rheumatoid arthritis, the general well being of the patients increased considerably, including an increase in body weight, muscle power and hemoglobin (one of the symptoms of rheumatoid arthritis is anemia).

Antibacterial, antiviral and antifungal activity

Tulsi leaves and essential oils possess antibacterial activity against staphylococci and other bacteria, as well as antiviral and antifungal activity. (See also **Liver protection** and **Encephalitis** section, above.)

Oral and periodontal health

Tulsi has traditionally been used as a treatment for halitosis and to strengthen gums and teeth. It is reported to cure mouth ulcers and pyorrhea/gum infections, and is considered very effective in toothache. Modern research offers empirical support for these traditional uses. Fresh Tulsi leaf extract shows preventive and therapeutic properties against human plaque cultures and oral infection.

Anabolic effect

An anabolic effect (enhancing protein synthesis) of Tulsi has been shown with in animal studies and suggested in human clinical research. This anabolic property may be useful in chronic diseases where marked destruction of protein and muscle occurs, such as tuberculosis, AIDS and malignomas.

Anti-insect effect

Tulsi impacts insects in two ways: (1) the juice and the essential oils of Tulsi leaves are insecticidal (e.g., against mosquitoes, ticks and their larvae); (2) Tulsi has insect repellent properties, reported by the British in 1904 and verified in modern studies. When Tulsi plants are grown, fewer mosquitoes are seen. In this respect, Tulsi can assist in the maintenance of a healthy human environment by reducing the likelihood of mosquito-born diseases.

Fertility issues

The question of the possible positive or negative effects of Tulsi on reproduction is one of the few areas where animal studies directly conflict with traditional Ayurvedic reports and human clinical experience. Several researchers have reported dose-dependent adverse effects of various Tulsi-based products on measures related to mouse and rat reproductive function. In contrast, traditional Ayurvedic references and reports, as well as modern clinical experience, would indicate the opposite outcome in humans. Several critical issues must be clarified before an explanation of this discrepancy can be presented.

Critical factors may include:

(1) *Interspecies differences.* Human and rodent reproduction systems may not be similar enough to support generalizations from one to the other.

(2) *Dosage.* Adverse effects were dose dependent; very high doses were needed to produce adverse effects in the rodent subjects. These would likely correspond with impractically large and highly unlikely quantities of Tulsi for human ingestion. Lower, more relevant doses did not produce significant changes in rodent reproductive measures.

(3) *Form and mode of administration.* Most animal studies involved the administration of extracts, although some employed large doses of whole Tulsi leaf compounded in the diet. Extracts are necessarily selective in what is extracted and

significantly alter the overall quantities and relative proportions of the various plant constituents. Consequently, they cannot reproduce the effects of the whole herb, which may contain counter-balancing or modulating components. One mouse study found adverse effects only with benzene and petroleum ether extracts, but not with a water-based extract (Batta and Santhakumari, 1971). This raises the question of the benzene and petroleum altering the structure and function of the natural constituents, resulting in the formation of toxic compounds. Furthermore, chemical solvents, such as benzene and petroleum ether may, themselves, cause problems in certain applications. It is generally very difficult to obtain an injectable form of plant extract that does not have negative effects. The intraperitoneal mode of administration, commonly used in animal studies, is particularly prone to adverse reactions that are not specific to the herbal constituents of primary interest.

Ayurvedic literature and European folklore is full of praise for Tulsi's profertile effects in men and women. Ancient texts like *Padmapurana* and *Garudapurana*, after centuries of observation on humans, describe Tulsi as a *child giver* and great *spermatogenic agent* (increasing the production of sperm) and report that Tulsi enhances the chances of women bearing progeny. Parts of the plant are reputed to have aphrodisiac effects (Vedvyasa, 1960; Vedavyasa, 1964; Shastri, 1968; Bhandari, 1970a, 1970b). We are inclined to give some credence to the experience of the ancient rishis, who based their belief on hundreds of years of observation and experience.

Our working assumption is that the vast majority of Tulsi animal study results (such as the adaptogenic/antistress, staminator, antioxidant, hepatoprotective, and immunomodulatory effects) likely generalize to humans, because of corresponding Ayurvedic reports and modern clinical experience, while the antifertile effects reported in rodents remain without evidence of relevance to humans.

In our clinical work, after prescribing Tulsi for fifteen years, we have observed no evidence of an antifertile effect in men or women. In fact, our experience has been the opposite. For example, in Case Study IV in *Appendix A*, we document the case of a young man in whom motility and count of sperm improved markedly with Tulsi treatment.

At this point, our professional view is that the animal antifertility studies cannot be generalized to normal human doses and patterns of use; rather we stand with our clinical experience and the ancient Ayurvedic use of Tulsi as a profertile agent in both men and women.

Nutritional value of Tulsi

Tulsi offers significant general health promoting nutritional qualities. The plant contains alkaloids, fats, carbohydrates, proteins, glycosides, saponins, tannins and essential oils (mainly terpenes and phenols) The leaves of Tulsi contain ascorbic acid (vitamin C), carotene (vitamin A), calcium, iron, and selenium, as well as zinc, manganese and sodium as trace elements. In addition, Tulsi is known to enhance digestion and absorption of other foods. Tulsi and related basil species are commonly used to improve the taste and nutrition of many food preparations around the world.

Whole herb medicine

Generally, the best way to use Tulsi is in its raw form. If fresh whole herbs are not available, we recommend herbs which are dried in the shade, or for short periods in the sun, and properly stored to preserve freshness and potency. We generally advocate the use of whole herbs so as to obtain the full synergistic interactive effects of the many bioactive constituents of the plant. Chemical extraction processes are necessarily selective, changing the balance of the herb's constituents and their activities, and may alter the active components. It is well recognized that pure synthetic drugs, as well as separate compounds isolated from plant extracts, are often more toxic than those in crude total plant form. Whole herb medicines generally have fewer side effects with better clinical acceptability, and offer nutritional as well as pharmacological support to the body.

We believe that nature provides the best medicine source on the planet. The human organism is generally better adapted to tolerate natural products than new synthetic substabces which are more foreign to the body. Modern allopathic drugs have only recently come into being, and are responsible for a significant number of iatrogenic (physician-induced) deaths and diseases. They must be used with considerable caution. We contend that natural products should provide the foundation for modern medical treatment.

Integration of traditional and modern health systems

In recognition of the many advantages of traditional/folk systems, in 1978 the World Health organization (WHO) recommended that traditional or folk healing be integrated wherever possible with modern scientific medicine, and stressed the necessity of ensuring rapport, recognition and collaboration among practitioners of the various systems. In the last two decades, there has been much fruitful effort in generating meaningful interaction between modern allopathic and alternative, traditional/folk medicine. Presently, however, various practices of modern and traditional systems are often mixed together on a hit-and-trial basis, without adequate progress in integrating the different approaches into an efficiently functioning whole. Ours is a serious effort to revitalize the herbal Ayurvedic system in the context of modern science and therapy, especially in areas of stress-related disease where modern medicines play a very limited role as preventive or curative agents.

Conclusion

Tulsi has many beneficial properties with negligible toxicity, and is an ideal antistress/ adaptogenic agent for the promotion of health and the prevention and treatment of disease. Life without health was well described by Herophilies in 300 BC (Robbins, 1987):

> *When health is absent*
> *Wisdom cannot reveal itself,*
> *Art cannot become manifest,*
> *Strength cannot be exerted,*
> *Wealth is useless and*
> *Reason is powerless.*

In conclusion, our prescription: "Use Tulsi and be healthy".

Appendix A
Case Reports from Dr. Narendra Singh's Clinic

I have been treating hundreds of patients successfully in the last few decades through herbs, especially Tulsi. Still, I am more and more in awe of Tulsi's healing power. Below are a few short sample case reports showing how Tulsi can function as a health and strength-improving agent – Dr. N. Singh.

Case I: Arterial hypertension

An elderly gentleman came to my clinic suffering from chronic arterial hypertension, which ran in the family. His blood pressure was initially 180 to 100 mm Hg (on average). On my advice he began taking two cups of Tulsi tea daily (some fresh leaves of Tulsi in freshly boiled water, infused for five minutes). His blood pressure dropped within one month to 160 to 90 mm Hg and in three months it dropped further to 120 to 70 mm Hg (on average), where it has maintained over the last 25 years. With this simple regime of two cups of Tulsi tea per day, now at the age of 82 years, his blood pressure is 120 to 65 mm Hg (on an average). Most of the male members of his family, including his father and his brother, died before the age of 60 years. He is a still healthy and feeling well, without any cardiac or other vascular problem. We attribute his good health and longevity, at least in part, to his regular daily habit of drinking Tulsi tea.

Case II: Osteoarthritis

A 58-year-old gentleman in the administrative services had osteoarthritis in both knee joints for three years. He had developed a marked weakness in his thighs and calves and suffered from pain and swelling of the knees. When he came into my clinic, I gave him a herbal antiarthritic formulation (containing Motha, Ashwagandha, Mulethi and Rama Tulsi) and the joint pain and swelling soon disappeared. However, his muscular weakness remained, which caused him great difficulty in walking. I added two capsule (300mg each) daily of dried powered Tulsi leaves to his medication and this produced a remarkable reduction in weakness within one month. He continued the treatment for a year and then discontinued it. Now it is more than two years since he stopped the treatment and his muscle power and health are still normal. We have never observed such results being attained by any synthetic drugs.

Case III: Urinary disorder

A lady of 55 years complained of having to urinate almost every hour. This made her social life very difficult and she was under a lot of mental stress. All other organ systems of the body showed no dysfunction. There was no diabetes mellitus, hormonal imbalance, or disease of urethra, bladder, ureters or kidneys detected through the usual blood and technical tests or physical examination. The modern allopathic drugs given by various previous physicians had no beneficial effect on her condition. Ultimately, she came to my clinic for herbal treatment. I suspected a problem of the pituitary gland, that was too subtle a disturbance (sub-clinical) to show up in the usual tests (the pituitary gland produces the antidiuretic hormone that prevents excessive loss of water by the body). I gave her one capsule of 300mg of dried powdered Tulsi leaves twice daily for 15 days. To my amazement, she came back on the 15th day telling me that she had no problem at all for the first time in six years. She would urinate only four to five times per day and was extremely happy to be able to lead a normal social life, including visits to friends, shopping and attending social functions and entertainment without her former problem. She continued the treatment with Tulsi for four months, discontinued it two months ago, and is now free of her problem. Modern scientific knowledge cannot yet explain how the dysfunction ceased, but the results are quite apparent. Perhaps the mechanism of action by which Tulsi achieved this effect will be understood one day in the future.

Case IV: Sexual impotence

In January 2001, a young man, age 28 years, visited our clinic complaining of sexual impotence. He and his wife had infrequent sexual relations and produced no children during their 8 years of marriage. Before our treatment began, the patient was advised to take no medicine for potency for a period of one month and then, after refraining from sexual activity for at least four days, have his semen examined at an independent laboratory.

On February 18, this baseline spermatozoa analysis revealed:

total sperm count	79.7 million/ml
progressively motile	15%
non-progressively motile	15%
non-motile	70%
morphologically abnormal	4% (giant headed)

Two days later he began treatment consisting of two 300 mg capsules of dried Tulsi leaves twice daily, resulting in a total daily dose of 1.2gm (approximately equal to 10-12gms of fresh leaves).

After a period of a little over two months, his semen was again examined, revealing:

total sperm count	146.8 million/ml
progressively motile	50%
non-progressively motile	20%
non-motile	30%
morphologically abnormal	10% (giant headed)

Following an additional month of Tulsi treatment, the semen was tested again revealing:

total sperm count	108.2 million/ml
progressively motile	65%,
non-progressively motile	20%,
non-motile	15%,
morphologically abnormal	6% (giant headed)

On March 16, after a period of more than one year Tulsi use, the semen was again examined, revealing:

total sperm count	126.9 million/ml
progressively motile	70%,
non-progressively motile	15%,
non-motile	15%,
morphologically abnormal	5% (giant headed)

In summary, after two months of treatment with Tulsi leaves there was a substantial increase in total sperm count and percent of progressively motile sperm and a decrease in non-motile sperm. These benefits were sustained over the following year with regular Tulsi use. Furthermore, the patient reported an increase in libido and sexual potency. No adverse side effects of any kind were detected. This case provides clear support for the safe profertile effects of Tulsi described in the traditional Ayurvedic literature.

Appendix B
Recommendations for Tulsi Capsules and Tea

Tulsi dosage schedule

For health promotion and prevention of disease: 1 capsule (300mg) of dried Tulsi leaves twice daily (600mg total) for at least 6 months.

For treatment of specific health disorders: 2-6 capsules per day (600-1800mg) for a period of 2 months to 1 year depending on the chronicity and severity of disease, and the general health status of the individual.

These benefits can also be readily obtained through the consumption of Tulsi tea (e.g., 1-5 cups per day) – taken separately or in combination with capsules. Tulsi can be beneficially consumed as a general health tonic for all ages throughout the life span.

Preparation and use of Tulsi tea (chai)

Tulsi can be readily brewed and taken as a particularly good-tasting herbal tea or chai, unlike many medicinal herbs which are not pleasant or convenient to prepare or consume. Tulsi in tea form has the additional, secondary benefits of being compatible with socializing and, compared to the consumption of capsules, may have more positive connotations, since it is less likely to be seen as taking medicine or pills.

The different varieties of Tulsi have notably different aromas and flavors that may include hints of lemon, clove, anise and peppermint. Tulsi can be prepared singly, as a blend of Tulsi varieties, or in combination with other herbs, spices, sweeteners, lemon or milk, for varying tastes and/or medicinal benefits. Combinations may include ginger (*Adrak*), lemon grass (*Sera*), licorice (*Mulethi*), gotu kola (*Brahmi*), as well as other herbs, common masala chai spices, and regular black or green tea. Natural sweeteners, such as jaggery (*gur*) or unboiled honey, may contribute desirable effects of their own – unlike refined white sugar, which should be avoided. Tulsi tea can be prepared from fresh or dried leaf and served hot or cold.

The following is a simple procedure for preparing Tulsi tea:

1. Bring fresh water to boil and turn off the burner.

2. Add one teaspoon or tea bag of dried Tulsi leaf per cup.

3. Infuse for two - five minutes or more. A longer steeping time yields a stronger infusion with more beneficial properties, although the tea may become a little bitter as a result. Covering during lengthy brewing helps reduce the loss of beneficial volatile constituents.

Appendix C
Tulsi use by the elderly

In this section we focus on the unique properties of Tulsi in maintaining the health of the elderly - and, in particular, the positive role of Tulsi tea. While Tulsi offers significant benefits for people of all ages, special challenges arise with aging to which Tulsi offers particular support.

Aging is a natural phenomena accompanied by degenerative changes in many physical and mental areas. It is primarily a genetically determined process, at the core of which is a slow diminution in the vitality of three basic biological systems characterized by:

- Reduced protein synthesis, and RNA and DNA deterioration.

- Reduced cell-mediated immunity.

- Reduced levels of hormones, neuro-transmitters and enzymes.

Although aging is genetically programmed, and obviously inevitable, environmental factors play a major role in delaying the aging process or, on the other hand, inducing unnecessary premature aging and ill health. Physical, biological and emotional stressors reduce biological resilience and speed up the aging process – and generally have increasing impact with age. These stressors typically trigger more adverse reactions in older people than in the young. Tulsi offers unique support to the body and mind in reducing the negative effects of these aging factors.

Old age commonly manifests poor health in the form of:

- *Low energy and easy fatigability*: Tulsi enhances endurance, increases the body's efficiency in using oxygen and aids cellular metabolism.

- *Insomnia*: Tulsi reduces emotional stress and has a calming effect.

- *Loss of muscle strength and co-ordination*: Tulsi has anabolic effects, improving protein synthesis and muscular strength.

- *Reduced digestive efficiency*: Elderly people commonly suffer from varying degrees of malnutrition resulting from reduced appetite and poor diet, and/or inefficient digestion and absorption of nutrients available in food consumed. Tulsi provides numerous valuable nutrients in readily absorbable, bioavailable form, as well as stimulating more efficient digestion of ingested food.

- *Increased susceptibility to infection*: Tulsi has general immunomodulating effects, as well as having specific antibacterial, antiviral and antifungal properties.

- *A variety of mental disturbances*, including memory loss, confusion, fear and anxiety and depression. Tulsi reduces emotional stress, has a calming effect and helps regulate hormones and neurotransmitters.

- *Stress-diseases* such as arthritis, hypertension, atherosclerosis and strokes, diabetes, dementia (e.g., Alzheimer's syndrome), asthma, cancer and other degenerative disorders. Tulsi has general adaptogenic/antistress effects that enhance the body's natural ability to resist disease and restore normal healthy function.

Many older people suffer from a variety of age and stress-related physical disorders and typically take a range of allopathic drugs in an attempt to manage the symptoms and progression of their degenerative problems. While often providing some relief, such drugs commonly bring with them a serious and well-acknowledged array of unpleasant and frequently dangerous adverse side effects - which may result in additional drug treatment to counteract, compensate for, or minimize the problems caused by the primary treatment drugs…and so on, often cascading into multiple drug use.

Tulsi may be helpful in reducing the risks and problems associated with allopathic

medicines and, having general adaptogenic and other health promotion qualities, may effectively serve as a complement or supplement to modern drugs. Furthermore, Tulsi's salutary effects on the disease process and the body's defense systems may enable a reduction in drug dose, with a corresponding decrease in adverse side effects.

Elderly people often suffer from worry, regrets and other mental and emotional stress-related disturbances resulting from a variety of factors, including their particular living conditions in modern society, their physical deterioration and their undeniable position at the latter end of the natural lifecycle. Many find the unavoidable loss of deceased life-long friends and loved ones highly stressful, and have difficulty accepting other rapidly changing environmental and cultural aspects of modern society. There is increasing social isolation of the elderly, and many find themselves living outside of the normal family context - often alone or in institutional settings. Some of these social problems are reflected in the quote below:

Old people require a life support system. That is why there are old people homes in advanced countries. Breaking down of old moral values for respecting, loving and caring for the old people and absence of the family support which existed in earlier times - old people's homes are the result. These are so-called homes but have no homely atmosphere. Homely atmosphere consisted of children and grandchildren playing with fathers and grandfathers, ladies of the house looking after everything for the young and the old. This natural atmosphere is missing today for old people in India and other developing countries. Also old people are getting segregated and separated from their families as their people leave them alone for their own interests. They are highly stressed people. Many of them are sick without a sickness.

As noted previously, in addition to providing health promoting pharmacological and nutritional adaptogenic/antistress effects, Tulsi taken in tea form is a simple pleasure that is conducive to socializing, which may in itself be beneficial to the elderly. And enjoying a pleasant cup of tea has positive connotations compared to the consumption of capsules, and is less likely to be seen simply as taking medicine or pills for illness.

Glossary of medical and other scientific terms

Abscess *n.* a localized collection of pus in any part of the body.

Adaptogen *n.* 1. agent that increases the body's ability to adapt to environmental and internal stress by strengthening the immune, nervous and glandular system. Enhances an organism's resistance to stress, disease and environment, as well as normalizes **metabolic** functions and increases metabolic efficiency. 2. A prophylactic, which heightens in an unspecific way the resistance of the organism to various environmental influences and stimuli and/or reduces the disposition or susceptibility to illness. 3. Enhances the body's nonspecific resistance to external stress or to noxious effects of physical, chemical or biological nature. - **adaptogenic** *adj.*

Adrenal glands a pair of suprarenal glands, constituted of **adrenal cortex**: outer portion of the gland, which produces the *corticosteroids* (cortico: belonging to the cortex**) hormones**, including **cortisol (hydrocortisone)**, **cortisone** and **aldosterone** and **adrenal medulla**: inner portion, which synthesizes, stores and releases **norepinephrine** and **epinephrine**.

Adrenaline *n.* see **epinephrine**.

AIDS (Acquired Immunodeficiency Syndrome) *n.* disease of the immune system suppresses the body's immune response. The current opinion is that AIDS is caused by HIV_1 or HIV_2 viruses (**H**uman **I**mmunodeficiency **V**irus) transmitted by exchange of body fluids, blood and semen. **T4 helper - inducer lymphocytes** are depleted due to the virus. Symptoms of earlier stage of **infection** include general involvement of the **lymph glands**, fever, weight loss and **diarrhea** (called **AIDS-related complex: ARC**). In later stages, various diseases occur due to the breakdown of the immune system (infections, cancer etc.).

Alkaloids *n.* group of nitrogen-containing substances that are produced by plants and have potent effect on body function. Many alkaloids are important drugs including **morphine**.

Allergen *n.* a substance that produces symptoms of **allergy** - can be food, feather, dust, pollen, bee sting, drugs etc.

Allergic shock *n.* see **anaphylactic shock**. Condition associated with collapse of the circulatory system. Produced by an **allergen**.

Allergy *n.* disorder in which the body becomes hypersensitive to particular **antigens** and provokes certain reactions (from hay fever, **asthma, dermatitis** to **allergic shock**). – **allergic** *adj.*

Amebiasis *n.* infection with ameba, especially *Entamoeba histolytica*, a minute acellular protozoan form of life found in soil and water, this **parasite** causes **inflammation** of the intestines with bloody **diarrhea** and cramps.

Anabolic *n.* increasing the **metabolic** process, promoting tissue growth.

Analgesia *n.* treatment of pain by painkillers (**analgesic:** drug that relieves pain).

Anaphylactic shock *adj.* a sudden severe **allergic** reaction characterized by hypotension, urticaria and breathing difficulties due to injection of foreign, allergenic substance like drug or bee venom into the body after a person has been sensitized.

Anatomy *n.* study of the structure of living organisms.

Anemia *n.* deficiency of red blood cells, **hemoglobin** or both.

Angiography *n.* X-Ray examination of the blood vessels.

Anoxia *n.* lack or absence of oxygen. Condition of the body in which the tissues are suffering from lack or absence of oxygen. - **anoxic** *adj.*

Antiarthritic *adj.* against **arthritis.**

Antibacterial *adj.* destroying or stopping the growth of bacteria.

Antibiotic *n.* a substance that inhibits the growth of, or destroys the bacteria or other microorganisms.

Anticarcinogen *n.* an agent that prevents, inhibits, diminishes and/or destroys malignant tumors. - **anticarcinogenic** *adj.*

Anticoagulant *n.* an agent that prevents the clotting of blood and platelet aggregation.

Anticoagulase *n.* enzyme preventing the coagulation of the blood.

Antidiabetic *adj.* an agent that prevents or relieves diabetes, an adjuvant in the treatment of **diabetes mellitus**.

Antifungal *adj.* an agent that destroys or inhibits the growth of fungi.

Antigen *n.* a substance that stimulates the production of **antibodies** - toxins, bacteria, foreign blood cells and cells of transplanted organs.

Anti-inflammatory *adj.* a drug reducing **inflammation** (like **glucocorticoids, NSAIDs**). Inflammation reducing.

Antioxidant *n.* an agent that prevents damage to cells by inhibiting **oxidation** and neutralizing **free radicals;** converting **lipid peroxides** into harmless molecules. Antioxidants are produced in the cells, decline with age, wrong nutrition and stress. For example **vitamin C, beta-carotene,** vitamin E, are Antioxidants. - **Antioxidant** *adj.*

Antiparasitic adj. against **parasites**

Antipyretic *n.* an agent that reduces or prevents fever.

Antistress agent *n.* preventing or reducing the ill effects of stress, a pharmacological term coined by Dr. Narendra Singh and co-workers. - **antistress** *adj.*

Antitubercular *adj.* against **tuberculosis**.

Antiviral *adj.* a substance that inhibits the growth of a virus.

Aplastic anemia *n.* **anemia** due to bone marrow failure to produce red/ white blood cells and platelets.

Arterial hypertension *n.* high blood pressure due to increase in peripheral resistance resulting from vasoconstriction or narrowing of peripheral blood vessels.

Arthritis *n.* **inflammation** of the joints, with swelling, warmth, redness and restriction of movement. Eventually, deformation of the joints.

Ascorbic acid *n.* vitamin C, **Antioxidant** essential in maintaining healthy connective tissues and the integrity of the cell walls. Necessary for the synthesis of collagen.

Aspirin or acetylsalicylic acid *n.* an analgesic, also reduces fever, **inflammation** and reduces production of **prostaglandin**. Can cause **allergic** reactions, **gastric ulcers**.

Atherosclerosis *n.* disease of the arteries in which calcified atherosclerotic plaques form, lining the wall of arterial vessels, composed of various lipids, foam cells, scar tissue and overgrown smooth muscle cells from the arterial wall. First, through vitamin C deficiency, a crack forms in the arterial wall, **lipoprotein** (a) (a very effective leak plugger, special type of **LDL**) plugs the leak, gluing through other lipoproteins (LDL, bags of oxidized **cholesterol** and lipids) happens and then stimulation of the muscle cells of the arterial wall through lipoprotein (a) occurs and forms a swelling which causes obstruction of the arterial vessel.

Autoimmune disease with immune response of the body against its own tissues or types of cells.

Bacilli *n.* rod-shaped **bacteria** (singular: **bacillus**).

Benzene *n.* chemical solvent often used for the extraction of plant material.

Biliary colic (pain in waves) affecting the bile duct (between the **gall bladder** and the **duodenum**).

Bioavailability *n.* availability to a living system, like the human body.

Boils *n.* furuncles, an acute circumscribed **inflammation** of the subcutaneous layers of the skin, gland or hair follicle.

Botany *n.* the study of plants.

Bronchial asthma *n.* difficulty in breathing due to spasmodic contractions of the muscular walls of the bronchial tubes (**bronchi** and **bronchioles**) due to smooth muscle spasm, **inflammation** or **edema** of the bronchial mucous membrane and overproduction of mucous.

Bronchiole *n.* (*pl.* **bronchioles**) smaller bronchial tubes.

Bronchitis *n.* **inflammation** of mucous membrane of the bronchial tubes.

Bronchospasm *n.* smooth muscle spasm of the **bronchus** and **bronchiole** (subdivision of the bronchial tree, **bronchioles** *pl.*).

Cardio-depressant *n.* **cardio**: heart - an agent reducing contractility of the heart muscle.

Carotene *n.* plant pigment, occurring in several forms, one is **beta-carotene**, which is an antioxidant and can be converted in the body into vitamin A.

Cataract *n.* opacity in the lens of the eye; results in blurred vision.

Catarrh *n.* a condition of the mucous membranes, particularly those of the upper respiratory tract, including the sinuses and throat, characterized by **inflammation** and conspicuous, mainly mucinous discharge.

Cell-mediated (or cellular) immune response immune response to an **antigen**, mediated through the **T-lymphocytes**.

Cellular immune system part of the immune system, expressed through the **T-lymphocytes**.

Cerebral *n*. belonging to the brain.

Chloramphenicol *n*. antibiotic normally used only for severe **infectio1ns**, because of the possibility of severe side effects.

Cholesterol *n*. one of the two types of blood fats (the other ones are the **triglycerides**) carried in **lipoproteins**, which are globular packages that also contain proteins, known as **apoproteins**. Cholesterol is an essential element of all cell membranes and forms the backbone of **steroid hormones** and bile acids.

Caecum *n*. last part of the large intestine (colon) before the rectum and anus.

Coma *n*. state of unrousable unconsciousness.

Coryza *n*. acute rhinitis (**inflammation** of the mucous membrane of the nose).

Coronary heart disease *n*. atherosclerosis of the coronary arteries (supplying the blood to the heart).

Corticoid-like syndrome *n*. by overdose of **cortisone** treatment, **edema**, **insomnia** and **arterial hypertension** can occur, all symptoms of action of increased **cortisone** in the body. Ginseng in very high doses acts like a **corticoid**.

Corticosteroids *n*. steroid hormones produced by the **adrenal cortex**.

1. **Glucocorticoids** *n*. **hydrocortisone (cortisol), cortisone** and others, essential for the utilization of fat, carbohydrate and protein of the body and for normal

answer to stress.

2. **Mineralocorticoids** *n*. **aldosterone**, regulation of salt and water balance.

Cortisone *n*. **hormone** of the **adrenal cortex**. used to treat deficiency of **corticosteroid** hormones.

Cytotoxic *adj*. damaging or destroying cells.

Diabetes mellitus metabolic disorder marked by hyperglycemia (high blood sugar), polyuria, thirst, acidosis, wasting, weight loss, insufficient production of **insulin** by the **pancreas** (type 1), or decreased sensitivity of the cells to insulin (type 2), resulting in abnormal **metabolism** of carbohydrates, fats and proteins.

Diarrhea *n*. loose motions; abnormally frequent intestinal evacuations of unformed stools.

Diastolic *adj*. belonging to the **diastole** *n*. the period between two contractions of the heart, when the muscle of the heart relaxes. The diastolic blood pressure is the lowest during the diastole, when the ventricles are relaxing and refilling. See also **systolic**.

Diuretic *n*. an agent increasing excretion of urine.

Dopamine *n*. belongs to the **catecholamines**. A **neurotransmitter** formed by the brain, essential for normal functioning of the central nervous system.

Duodenum *n*. first part of the intestines.

Dysentery *n*. infectious **inflammation** of the mucous membrane of the intestines with **diarrhea**, abdominal pain, etc.

Dyspepsia *n*. discomfort in the lower chest due to indigestion.

Edema (oedema) *n*. abnormal excess of accumulation of serous fluids in connective tissue or in a serous cavity.

Electrolytes solution that produces ions; in medical terms it usually means the concentration of separate ions (like sodium, potassium etc.) in the circulating blood.

Encephalitis *n.* **inflammation** of the brain, mainly caused by viral or bacterial **infection** of the brain. **Japanese encephalitis type B**: Caused by arbovirus, transmitted by mosquitoes, in temperate East, southern and Southeast Asia.

Endothelial cells -cells lining the blood and lymphatic vessels as well as the heart from inside.

Enzymes *n.* special types of proteins with the ability to facilitate and speed up the rate of a chemical or biological reaction.

Eosinophil leukocytes *n.* type of white blood cells containing cytoplasmic granules easily stained by eosin (biological stain), involved in the body's response to **allergy**.

Epinephrine *n.* **adrenaline**— hormone secreted by the **adrenal medulla** and released into the bloodstream in response to stress, enables the body to "fright, fight or flight"; also a **neurotransmitter**.

Erythema *n.* redness of the skin, sign of **inflammation** or **infection**.

Essential oils essences of aromatic plants obtained by pressing, distillation or use of organic solvents.

Exacerbation *n.* "making worse; irritating." Acute outbreak of a chronic disease.

Expectoration *n.* removal of secretion of **bronchopulmonary** mucous membrane; causes the expulsion of mucus from the respiratory tract. **expectorant** adj.

Filariasis *n.* infection with *Wuchereria bancrofti*, threadlike nematode worms.

Forced vital capacity (fvc) the volume of gas that can be forcefully expelled from the lungs after maximal inspiration.

Free radicals *n.* during the process of **oxidation**, **free radicals** are formed. They are molecules with an extra unpaired electron and are highly reactive. If not neutralized, they continue to damage in a chain reaction. As an exception, **oxygen free radicals** are cleansing, assist in the breakdown of toxins and kill pathogenic organisms. **Hydroxyl free radicals** (from the breakdown of fats) destroy cell structures, particularly cell membranes. **Antioxidants** neutralize free radicals.

Gastric *adj.* pertaining to the stomach.

Giardiasis *n.* infection of the small intestine with the **parasitic** protozoa *Giardia lamblia*, acute or chronic **diarrhea**, often with nausea, weight loss, formation of intestinal gas and fatty stools.

Glucocorticoids or **glucosteroids** *n.* group of **steroid hormones**, produced by the **adrenal cortex**, involved in carbohydrate, fat and protein metabolism; **Anti-inflammatory** properties.

Glycosides *n.* organic compounds occurring abundantly in plants that yield one or more sugars among the products of hydrolysis.

Goitre *n.* struma, enlargement of the thyroid that is commonly visible as a swelling of the anterior part of the neck; may be due to **infections**, tumors, hyper - or hypofunction of the thyroid gland.

Gonorrhea *n.* a contagious **infection** of the urinogenital tract caused by Gonococcus bacterium, a sexually transmitted disease.

Helper T- cells *n.* see **T- cells**.

Hemoglobin *n.* substance contained within the red blood cells and responsible for their color; transports the oxygen in the blood, measured in g/dl.

Hemorrhage *n.* internal bleeding through profuse bleeding from the blood vessels.

- **hemorrhagic** *adj.*

Hepatitis *n.* **infection** of the liver by virus (amongst others are hepatitis A,B,C,D,E - virus, herpes simplex virus, cytomegalovirus, Epstein-Barr virus) or **inflammation** of the liver through drugs or toxic agents.

Hepato- *prefix.* **belonging** to the liver.

Hepatopathy disease of the liver.

Hernia *n.* the protrusion or projection of an organ or a part of an organ through the wall of the cavity that normally contains it.

HPA (hypothalamo-Pituitary-Adrenal axis) *n.* also called neuroaxis: Relation of **hypothalamus - pituitary gland (hypophysis) - adrenal glands.**

Humoral *adj.* belonging to the blood.

Humoral immunity *n.* function of the **B lymphocytes** (B-cells) producing free **antibodies** that circulate in the blood stream and deal with **antigens**, defending the immunity of the body.

5-Hydroxytryptamine *n.* also called **serotonin**, plays a role in sleep, **inflammation** and as a **neurotransmitter**.

Hyperlipidemia (LDL, HDL) *n.* too high blood fats, they are carried as **lipoproteins** and are suspended in the blood serum. They can only be separated by centrifugation. The most dense family of lipoproteins is called **HDL** (mainly **cholesterol** and apoproteins), less dense are the **LDL** (which carry most of the serum **cholesterol**).

1   **Low-density-lipoprotein (LDL)** *n.* high LDL level in the blood indicates greater risk of **coronary heart disease**.

2   **High-density-lipoprotein (HDL)** *n.* high HDL level in the blood indicates lower risk for coronary heart disease.

Hypermotile *adj.* over mobility, here used for the normal movement of the intestine to transport the food material forwards.

Hypo-and Hypercholesterolemia *n.* too high or low plasma **cholesterol** level.

Hypoglycemia *n.* low blood sugar.

Hypolipidemic *adj.* blood fat lowering.

Hypotension *n.* low blood pressure. - **hypotensive** *adj.*

Hypothalamus *n.* region of the forebrain at the floor of the third ventricle, linked with the thalamus above the **pituitary gland**, serves amongst others as a centre of integration of hormonal and autonomic nervous activity through its control of the pituitary secretions.

Iatrogenic *adj.* describing a condition that results from a treatment (physician/drug induced disease).

Ibuprofen *n.* non-steroidal anti-inflammatory drug (**NSAID**) used in treatment of **arthritis**.

Idiopathic *adj.* denoting a disease or condition, the cause of which is not known, or that arises spontaneously.

Immunomodulator *n.* an agent that regulates the humoral and cellular immune response, usually improving the immunity.

Induration *n.* abnormal hardening of a tissue or organ.

Infection *n.* invasion of the body by harmful organisms, such as bacteria, fungi, viruses etc.

Inflammation *n.* the body's response to injury, acute (immediate defensive action to **infection**, chemicals or physical agents) or chronic inflammation. - **inflammatory** *adj.*

Insomnia *n.* sleeplessness.

Intraperitoneal *adj.* inside or into the peritoneum.

Insulin *n.* a protein **hormone**, secreted by the beta cells of the **Islets of Langerhans** of the **pancreas;** maintains the blood sugar level in normal ranges. Lack of this hormone gives rise to diabetes mellitus.

Islets of Langerhans of the pancreas *n.* small group of cells scattered throughout the tissue of the **pancreas.** There are three main histological types of cells alpha, beta and delta cells; these cells produce glucagons, insulin and somatostatin hormones respectively.

Interstitial nephritis *n.* **inflammatory** disorder of the renal interstitium (connective tissue) in which the immune system plays a significant role pathogenetically.

Jaundice *n.* Yellowish appearance of the eyes and skin, evidence of accumulation of bilirubin (orange or yellow pigment produced by breakdown of the **hemoglobin**) in the body tissues, manifestation of liver disease.

Krebs cycle *n.* a complex cycle of enzyme – catalyze reactions, occurring within the cells of all living animals in which acetate, in presence of oxygen, is broken down to produce energy in the form of ATP and carbon dioxide. The cycle is the final stage of **oxidation** of fats, proteins and carbohydrates.

Leprosy *n.* a chronic mycobacterial disease that is sometimes infectious, affects primarily the nervous system and secondarily the skin and certain other tissues.

Leukopenia *n.* decreased number of white blood cells in the peripheral blood.

Leukocytes *n.* white blood cells which protect the body from **infection** and disease.

Leukoderma *n.* deficiency of pigmentation of the skin, usually occurring in patches.

Libido: sexual drive.

Lipid peroxidation *n.* **cholesterol** and fats (particularly unsaturated fats) are oxidized to become **free radicals,** called **peroxides. Lipid** (fat) **peroxides** attack and destroy cell membranes. **Antioxidants** convert lipid peroxides into harmless molecules.

Lymph *n.* the fluid similar in composition to plasma but contains less protein and some cells, mainly lymphocytes, present within the vessels of the lymphatic system.

Lymph gland or lymph nodes one of a number of small swellings found at intervals along the lymphatic system. They are composed of lymphoid tissue act as filters of the **lymph**, preventing foreign particles from entering the bloodstream.

Lymphocytes *n.* type of white blood cells, formed in lymphoid tissues (lymph nodes, spleen, **thymus** and tonsils), function in the development of immunity, include **B** and **T-cells.**

Mad cow disease *n.* disease of cows caused by the Cure virus; appeared first in Great Britain.

Malaria *n.* febrile disease caused by **infection** with a protozoan *Plasmodium*, transmitted by the bite of infected female mosquitoes of the genus Anopheles, characterized by cycles of chills and fever. - **malarial** *adj.*

Malignomas *n. pl.* cancerous tumors.

Maximum breathing capacity (mbc) the maximum volume of air that can be breathed into the lungs.

Mean *n.* statistical term: the average of a group of observations calculated by adding their values and dividing by the number in the group.

Metabolism *n.* the sum of all the chemical and physical changes that take place within the body and enable its growth and functioning. - **metabolic** *adj.*

Metabolites *n.* substances that take part in the metabolism.

Mitochondria *n. pl.* structure of the cytoplasm (jelly-like substance that surrounds the nucleus of the cell) of every cell that is the site of the cell energy production. - **mitochondrial** *adj.*

Morphine *n.* potent painkiller, used mainly to relieve severe and persistent pain.

Mucoproteins *n.* one of a group of proteins found in the blood globulins with a carbohydrate group.

Muscle necrosis death of muscle tissue.

Myocardial infarction infarction of the myocardium — the heart muscle, through occlusion of the coronary arteries, which supply blood for the heart muscle.

Nephritis, interstitial *n.* **inflammation** of the kidneys, especially of the connective tissue of the kidneys caused by **infection**, degeneration or vascular disease. The immune system is involved pathogenetically.

Neurotransmitters: Hormones responsible for the transmission of nerve impulses and transmission of information in the central nervous system.

Nonsteroidal-anti-inflammatories (or anti-inflammatory) drugs (NSAIDs) large group of drugs for pain relief. They inhibit the biosynthesis of **prostaglandins** (important mediators of **inflammation**) and inhibit to various degrees blood platelet aggregation. They include **aspirin** and **ibuprofen**.

Norepinephrine *n.* also called **noradrenaline**; **hormone** and **neurotransmitter** secreted by the **adrenal medulla** and the nerve endings of the sympathetic nervous system preparing the body for stress.

Nuclear medicine. branch of medicine concerned with radionuclides (radioactive atomic nucleus used to label tracers for diagnosis) in the study, diagnosis and treatment of disease.

Opium *n.* a narcotic drug made from the juice of the seed capsule of the opium poppy, used as an intoxicant and medicinally to relieve pain and produce sleep.

Opium receptors in the brain group of cells specialized to bind opium and trigger impulses in the central nervous system.

Osteoarthritis *n.* form of **arthritis** characterized by chronic degeneration of joint cartilage. Degenerative deformation sometimes combined with **inflammation** of joints.

Oxidation in medicine, burning of oxygen in the body. Chemically an oxidation reaction removes negative charges by removing electrons. Oxidation creates **free radicals**.

P<0.01. A statistical estimate of the likelihood that the difference found in a study could have occurred by chance alone. The probability of such a difference happening solely by chance is 1 in 100. Such a finding (**P<0.01**) is considered "statistically significant."

Pancreas *n.* a gland behind the stomach, which secretes digestive **enzymes**. A part of the pancreas is the **Islets of Langerhans**, interspersed among the other tissue. These isolated groups of cells secrete the **hormones insulin** and glucagon.

Parasite *n.* an organism that grows, feeds and is sheltered in or on another living organism, while contributing nothing to the survival of the host. Some parasites cause irritation and interfere with bodily functions; others destroy host tissues and release toxins into the body, thus injuring health and causing diseases. - **parasitic** *adj.*

Peristaltic *adj.* wavelike movement that progresses along some of the hollow tubes of the body, especially the intestinal walls.

Peritonitis *n.* **inflammation** or **infection** of the serous membrane (peritoneum) lining the abdominal cavity.

Petroleum ether: chemical solvent for extraction of plant materials.

Pharmacology *n.* science of the properties of drugs and their effect on the body. - **pharmacological** *adj.*

Phenols *n.* monohydroxyl derivates of benzene.

Physiology *n.* science of the functioning of living organisms. - **physiological** *adj.*

Piles (hemorrhoids) *n.* enlargement of the normal spongy blood filled cushions in the wall of the anus, usually a consequence of prolonged constipation or, occasionally, diarrhea.

Pituitary gland also called **hypophysis**, it is located in the brain and secretes several **hormones** with their respective actions, amongst them **ACTH**.

Platelet-aggregation-inhibitor agent inhibiting the aggregation (gathering) of the platelets of the blood (involved in blood clotting). For example, aspirin is a platelet-aggregation-inhibitor. It decreases the adhesiveness of the platelets by release of ADP (Adenosine diphosphate), a mediator of the second phase of platelet aggregation. In rare cases, it also causes severe thrombocytopenia.

Prednisone *n.* synthetic **corticosteroid** used to treat rheumatic diseases, severe **allergic reactions** and **inflammation** etc.

Prostaglandins *n.* **hormone**-like substances, present in many tissues and body fluids; can cause contraction of smooth muscle (for example, that of the uterus), mediators in the process of **inflammation** (**NSAID**s block their production), contribute to production of mucus in the stomach which provides protection against acid **gastric** juice.

Pulmonary *adj.* belonging to the lungs.

Radiotherapy *n.* treatment of disease with radiation like X-Rays or other radiation. Many forms of cancer are treated by radiotherapy.

Respiratory chain is present in the **mitochondria** of the cells and functions in cellular respiration (also called **tissue respiration**).

Rheumatoid arthritis autoimmune disease- a common form of chronic **inflammatory arthritis** of unknown cause, not associated with a known **infection**. Multisystem disease, characterized most often by sustained **inflammation** of multiple joints.

Saponins *n.* group of naturally occurring, nonpoisonous, oily glycosides that foam freely when shaken with water.

Schizophrenia *n.* psychotic disorder in perception and cognition characterized by delusion, hallucinations and a withdrawal from reality, accompanied by emotional, behavioral and intellectual disturbances.

Sedative *n.* an agent that exerts a soothing or **tranquilizing** effect, reducing anxiety, stress, irritability and excitement.

Serotonin *n.* also **5-Hydroxytryptamine** formed from tryptophan and found in the brain, blood serum, **gastric** mucosa, among other tissues. Vasoconstrictor that inhibits gastric secretion, also can act as a vasodilator, stimulates smooth muscle, inhibits pain pathways in the spinal cord, helps control moods, helps cause sleep.

Shock *n.* a state resulting from acute peripheral circulatory failure. It may occur following **haemorrhage**, severe trauma, surgery, burns, dehydration, **infections**, drug toxicity or **allergy**, also includes **hypotension**, **cyanosis**, and urinary retention.

Spermatogenic inducing the formation of spermatozoa or sperm.

Sphincter *n.* a specialized ring of muscles that surround an orifice.

Sphincter ani the sphincter at the lower ending of the alimentary canal. **Ani** - *prefix.* for anus.

Sputum *n.* material coughed up from the respiratory tract.

Standard deviation in statistics, a measure of the scatter of observations about their arithmetic **mean.**

Staphylococci *n. pl.* genus of bacteria, causing boils and **abscesses.**

Steroids *n.* class of naturally occurring or synthetic fat-soluble organic compounds, **adrenal hormones**, sexual hormones, **saponins** etc.

Stimulants *n.* agents that promote the activity of the body system or function. Amphetamine and caffeine are stimulants of the central nervous system.

Syphilis *n.* chronic contagious disease sexually transmitted by the bacteria *Treponema pallidum.*

Systolic *adj.* belonging to the **systole** *n.* the period of the cardiac cycle during which the ventricles (the heart chambers) contract and in which the blood pressure is the highest. The blood pressure is the pressure of the blood against the walls of the arteries. Blood pressure is measured in millimeters of mercury (mm Hg). The normal is around 120 mm Hg.

Tachycardia *n.* fast heart rate - in adults above 100 per minute.

Tannins *n.* group of simple and complex phenol, polyphenol and flavonoid compounds bound with starch.

T-cells *n.* subgroup of the **lymphocytes**, matures in the **thymus** gland, then are located in the lymphoid tissues. They are involved in the **cell-mediated immune response** of the body. Several subpopulations: **Helper-inducer T cells** (also called **CD4** or **T4**), killer T-cells, suppressor T- cells and inducer T- cells.

Terpenes *n.* any of a group of unsaturated hydrocarbons, many of which are found in plant oils and resins and are responsible for the scent of plants. Larger terpenes include vitamin A.

Thrombocyte (platelet) *n.* a disc-shaped cell structure in the blood, involved in blood clotting.

Thrombocyte-aggregation-inhibitors. Thrombocytes clot blood through aggregation; these drugs inhibit the process of blood clotting. **e.g., aspirin**

Thrombocytopenia *n.* abnormal decrease in the number of platelets in the circulating blood.

Thrombosis *n.* a condition in which the blood forms a clot (thrombus) and can obstruct the blood flow. - **antithrombotic** *adj.* against thrombosis.

Thymus *n.* gland sitting above and in front of the heart. Site of the **T–lymphocytes**, involves with age.

Tissue respiration cellular respiration; involves the **respiratory chain**, series of **enzymes** and proteins in the living cell through which electrons are transferred. This leads to conversion of chemical energy into a readily usable and storable energy.

Tranquilizers *n.* drug that produces a calming effect, relieving anxiety and tension. - **tranquilizing** *adj.*

Triglycerides *n.* second of the two classes of blood fats (the other one being **cholesterol**), carried by the **lipoproteins**. See cholesterol. The triglycerides are involved in transforming energy from food into the cells.

Tuberculoid leprosy *n.* a chronic infectious disease by the *Mycobacterium leprae*, which involves skin, nerves, nose, eyes, etc. In the tuberculoid subtype, the immunity of the person is intact and the course is more benign with discoloration of the skin and numbness.

Tubercular *n.* having small round swellings; usually adjective of tuberculosis.

Tuberculosis *n.* an acute or chronic disease, highly variable, communicable, caused by the tubercle bacillus, especially of the lung tissue, spreads from local lesions or by way of the **lymph** or blood vessels. Symptoms include fever, night sweats, and loss of weight.

Ulcer *n.* **gastric** and **duodenal** - a depressed, well-defined area of excavation into the deeper layers of an organ; gastric: into the mucous membrane of the stomach, duodenal: into the mucous membrane of the duodenum.

Virocidal *n.* destroys viruses.

Bibliography

Adam, U.S. Oceanite: *A Maritime Union of India Publication*, **1997**, *197*:37.

Agarwal, P., Rai, V and Singh, B.B. Randomized placebo controlled, single blind trial of basil leaves in patients with NIDDM. *Proc. World Cong. Biotech. Dev. Med. Sub. Plant and Marine Origin. K.G.M.C. Lucknow*, **1995**, pp. 87.

Agarwal, P., Rai, V. and Singh, R.B. Randomized placebo-controlled, single blind trial of holy basil leaves in patients with noninsulin-dependent diabetes mellitus. *Int. J. Clin. Pharmacol. Ther.*, **1996**, *34(9)*:406-409.

Anonymous. *The Wealth of India*, Raw materials (N-P) CSIR Publication, New Delhi. **1966**, 7:88-91.

Anonymous. Tulsi. In: *The Ayurvedic System of Medicine (Pharmacopeia)*, **1820**, II (Part I & II).

Aruna, K. and Sivaramakrishnan, V.M. Anticarcinogenic effects of some Indian plant products. *Food Chem. Toxicol.*, **1992**, *30(11)*:953-956.

Aruna, K. and Sivaramakrishnan, V.M. Plant products as protective agents against cancer. *Ind. J. Exp. Biol.*, **1990**, *28(11)*:1008-1011.

Atal, C.K., Sharma, M.L., Kaul, A. and Khajuria, Immunomodulating agents of plant origin. I: Preliminary screening. *J. Ethnopharmacol.*, **1996**, *18(2)*:133-141.

Balanehru, S. and Nagarajan, B. Intervention of adriamycin induced free radical damage. *Biochem. Int.*, **1992**, *28(4)*:735-744.

Balanehru, S. and Nagarajan, B. Protective effect of oleanolic acid and ursolic acid against lipid peroxidation. *Biochem. Int.*, **1991**, *24(5)*:981-990.

Banu, M.J., Nellaiappan, K. and Dhandayuthapani, S. Mitochondrial malate dehydrogenase and malic enzyme of a filarial worm *Setaria digitata*: some properties and effects of drugs and herbal extracts. *Jpn. J. Med. Sci. Biol.*, **1992**, *45(3)*:137-150.

Bansi, L. Bradu, Pushpangadan, P. and Kaul, B. L. Screening and development of new aroma chemicals from genetic resouces of genus *Ocimum. J. Med. Aro. Plant Sci.*, **2000**, *22*:411-418.

Bataru, N.C., Tania, U.N., Negrao, B.E.M.A.F., Gracia, C.D.A. and Dias, F.B.P. Antibacterial activity of *Ocimum gratissimum* L. essential oil. *Mem. Inst. Osweldo Cruz*, **1999**, *94*:675-678.

Batta, S.K. and Santhakumari, G. The antifertility effect of *Ocimum sanctum* and *Hibiscus rosa sinensis*. *Ind. J. Med. Res.*, **1971**, *59*:777.

Bhandari, C.R. Tulsi *(Ocimum sanctum)*. In: *"Vanaushadhi Chandroday" (An Encyclopedia of Indian Herbs)*. Publisher: CS Series of Varanasi Vidyavilas Press, Varanasi, India, **1970a**, *5*:32-39.

Bhandari, C.R. Tulsi *(Ocimum gratissimum)*. Ibid **1970b**, *1*:78-79.

Bhargava, K.P. and Singh, N. Anti-stress activity of *Ocimum sanctum* (Linn.). *Ind. J. Med. Res.*, **1981**, *73*:443- 451.

Bhargava, K.P. and Singh, N. Comparative evaluation of anti-stress activity of Eleutherococcus senticosus, Panax ginseng and Ocimum sanctum. New Data on Eleutherococcus. *Proc. IInd Int. Symp. Eleutherococcus Moscow (U.S.S.R)*, **1984**, pp. 181-89.

Bhargava, K.P. and Singh, N. Indian plants as anti-stress agents. *Proc. International Research Congress. Natural Product College Pharmacy, University North Carolina.USA*, **1985**, Abstract 202.

Bhat, J.V. and Broker, R.J. Anticoagulase factors in some indigenous plants. *Sci. Ind. Res.*, **1954**, *138(4)*:305.

Bhat, J.V. and Broker, R.J. Action of some plant extracts on pathogenic Staphylococci. *J. Sci. Ind. Res.*, **1955**, *128(11)*:540-542.

Brekhman I.I. Personal communication to Dr. N. Singh, **1983**.

Brekhman, I.I. and Dordymov, I.V. New substances of plant origin which increase non-specific resistance. *Ann. Rev. Pharmacol.*, **1969**, *9*:419.

Buckingham, J.C. Stress and the Neuroendocrine-Immune Axis: The pivotal role of glucocorticoids and lipocortin 1. Fifteenth Gaddum Memorial Lecture December 1994. *Brit. J. Pharmacol.*, **1996**, *118*:1-19.

Carak, Chikitsa Sthana Section of Therapeutics. In: *Carak Samhita*. Ayurvedic society of India, **1949**, *3*:1278.

Chavan, S.R. and Nikam, S.T. Mosquito larvicidal activity of *Ocimum basilicum* Linn. *Ind. J. Med. Res.*, **1982**, *75*:220-222.

Chopra, R.N., Nayar, S. I. and Chopra, I. C. *Glossary of Indian Medicinal Plants*. (CSIR), New Delhi, **1956.**

Chopra, R.N., Nayar, S.L. and Chopra, I.C. *Ocimum sanctum* In: *Glossary of Indian Medicinal Plants*. Pub. & Print. National Institute of Science Communication Dr. K.S. Krishnan Marg, New Delhi, **1996**, pp. 179.

Chopra, R.N., Roy, D.N. and Ghosh, S.M. Insecticidal and larvicidal action of the essential oils of the *Ocimum basilicum* and *Ocimum sanctum*. *J. Malaria. Inst. India*, **1941**, *4*:109.

Das, S.K., Chandra, A., Agarwal, S.S. and Singh, N. *Ocimum sanctum* (Tulsi) in the treatment of viral encephalitis (a preliminary clinical trial). *The Antiseptic*, **1983**, pp. 1-5.

Dash, B and Kashyap, L. Tridosha Concept, Introduction In: *Materia Medica of Ayurveda Based On Ayurveda Saukhyam Of Todarnanda*. Concept Publishing Company, New Delhi, India, **2000**, pp. 39.

Deshpande, R.S. and Tipnis, H.P. Insecticidal activity of *Ocimum basilicum*, Linn. *Pesticides*, **1977**, *11(5)*:11-12.

Devi, P.U., Bisht, K.S. and Vinitha, M. A comparative study of radioprotection by Ocimum flavonoids and synthetic aminothiol protectors in the mouse. *Brit. J. Radiol.*, **1998**, *71(847)*:782-784.

Dixit, K.S. and Singh, N. An assessment of immunomodulator activity of some anti-stress Indian plants. *Proc. Xth Int. Cong. Pharmacol. Sydney, Australia*, **1987**, *1*:265.

Dixit, K.S. Singh, S.P. Sinha, K.N. Singh, N. and Kohli, R.P. *Inula racemosa* (puskarmul), *Terminalia belerica* (Bibhitaka) and *Ocimum sanctum* (Tulsi)- A preliminary clinical trial in Asthma patients. *Proc. Int. Sem. Clin. Pharmacol. Dev. Count. K.G.M.C, Lucknow, India.* **1986**, *2*:22–27.

Dixit, K.S., Srivastava, M., Srivastava, A.K., Singh, S.P. and Singh, N. Effect of *Ocimum sanctum* on stress induced alterations upon some brain neurotransmitters and enzyme activity. *Proc. XVIIIth Ann. Conf. I.P.S., JIMPER, Pondichery,* **1985**, pp. 57.

Duke, J. and Duke, P. Tempest in the teapot: Mints. *Quart. J. Crude Drug Res.,* **1978**, *16(2)*:71-95.

Dutt, S. Chemical examination of the essential oil of *Ocimum sanctum. Ind. Acad. Sci.,* **1939**, pp. 72-77.

Dwivedi, S., Gupta, D. and Sharma, K.K. Modification of coronary risk factors by medicinal plants. *J. Med. Aro. Plant Sci.* **2000**, *22*:616-620.

Dymock, W., Warden, C.J.H. and David Hooper. *Ocimum sanctum* In:*Pharmacographia Indica, A History of Principal Drugs of Vegetable Origin.* London: Kegan Paul, Trench, Trubner & Co. Ltd., **1893**, *3*:86.

Fulder, S.J. Ginseng and the hypothalamic-pituitary control of stress. *Am. J. Chinese Med.,* **1981**, *9*:112-118.

Ganasoundari, A., Zare, S.M. and Devi, P.U. Modification of bone marrow radiosensitivity by medicinal plant extracts. *Brit. J. Radiol.,* **1997**, *70(834)*:599-602..

Garg, G.R. *Bhagavat, Mahabharat* and *Vishnupurana* by Maharshi Vedavyasa. In: *An Encyclopedia of Indian Literature.* Pub-Mittal Publisher, **1982**, pp. 313-316.

Godbole, S.R., Pendse, G.S. and Bedekar, V.A. *Glossary of vegetable drugs. Vagbhata.* Published by: Indian Drug Research Association, Pune, **1966**, pp. 145-146.

Godhwani, S., Godhwani, J.L. and Vyas, D.S. *Ocimum sanctum*: an experimental study evaluating its anti-inflammatory, analgesic and antipyretic activity in animals. *J. Ethnopharmacol.,* **1987**, *21(2)*:153-163.

Godhwani. S., Godhwani, J.L. and Vyas, D.S. *Ocimum sanctum*—a preliminary study evaluating its immunoregulatory profile in albino rats. *J. Ethnopharmacol.,* **1988**, *24(2-3)*:193-198.

Griffith, R.T.H. *The Hymns of the Rigveda.* Vidyavilas Press Limited, Varanasi, India, **1963**, *1*.

Grover, G.S. and Rao, J.T. Investigation on the antimicrobial efficiency of essential oils from *Ocimum sanctum* and *Ocimum gratissimum. Perfum Kosmet.,* **1977**, *58(11)*:326.

Gupta, K.C. and Vishwanathan. A short note on Antitubercular substance from *Ocimum sanctum. Antibiotic and Chemotherapy,* **1955**, *5*:33.

Gupta, R.S. Trial cultivation of some medicinal and aromatic plants in Malwa Region of M.P. Part II, Analysis of essential oils. *Indian Perfumer.,* **1987**, *31*:370-374.

Hooker, J.D. *Ocimum sanctum* In: *Flora of British India.* London: L. Reeve & Co., 5, Henrietta Street, Covent Garden. Bishen Singh, Mahendra Pal Singh. 23-A New Connaught Place Deharadun, India, 1982, Printed in India at Jayyad Press, Ballimaran, Delhi, **1885**, *4*:609.

Jain, S.R. and Jain, M.L Investigations on the essential oils of *Ocimum basilicum. Planta Med.,* **1973**, *24*:286.

Jalil, A. Clinical trial of *Ocimum sanctum* (Tulsi) in peptic ulcer and hyperacidity patients. *J. Res. Ind. Med.,* **1970**, *4(2)*:238-239.

Jogetia, G.C., Devi, U., Singhatgeri, M.K., Singh, N. and Kohli, R.P. Radiation modifying effects of *Ocimum sanctum* on mouse survived. *Proc. Ind. Sci. Cong.,* Jaipur. **1986**, pp. 20.

Kalsi, R., Singh, N. and Gupta, G..P. Effects of stress and anti-stress drugs on succinate dehydrogenase enzyme (SDH) in rat brain (A possible role of SDH in stress adaptation phenomenon). *Physiology of Human Performance. Proc. Nat. Symp. Physiol. Hum. Perfor.* (Sawhney, R.C., Sridharan, K. and Selvamurthy, W. eds) Publisher: Defence Institute of Physiology and Allied Sciences, Defence Research and Development Organization (DRDO), Govt. of India, Delhi, **1987**, pp. 114-117.

Karthikeyan, K., Ravichandran, P. and Govindasamy, S. Chemopreventive effect of *Ocimum sanctum* on DMBA-induced hamster buccal pouch carcinogenesis. *Oral Oncol.,* **1999**, *35(1)*:112-119.

Kashinathan, S., Ramakrishnan, S. and Basu, S. Antifertility effects of *Ocimum sanctum* Linn. *J. Exp. Biol.,* **1972**, *10(1)*:23-25.

Kaul, V.K. and Nigam, S.S. Antibacterial and antifungal studies of some essential oils. *J. Res. Ind. Med. Yoga and Homeo.,* **1977**, *12(3)*:132-135.

Kelm, M.A. and Nair, M.G. Mosquitocidal compounds and a triglyceride, 1,3-dilinoleneoyl-1-palmitin, from *Ocimum sanctum. Jour. Agri. Food Chem.,* **1998**, *46*:3092-3094.

Khanna, S., Gupta, S.R. and Grover, J.K. Effect of long term feeding of Tulsi (*Ocimum sanctum* Linn) on reproductive performance of albino rats. *Ind. J. Expt. Biol.* **1986**, *24*:302-304.

Khurana, M.L and Vagikar, M.B. *Ocimum basilicum* Part I - A chemical study of the oil. *Ind. J. Pharm.,* **1950**, *12(5)*:132-133.

Khurana, M.L. and Vagikar, M.B. *Ocimum basilicum* Part II - Antibacterial properties. *Ind. J. Pharm.,* **1959**, *12(5)*:134-135.

Kim, O.K., Murakami, A., Nakamura, Y. and Ohigashi, H. Screening of edible Japanese plants for nitric oxide generation inhibitory activities in RAW 264.7 cells. *Cancer Lett.,* **1998**, *125(1-2)*:199-207.

Kirtikar, K.R. and Basu, B.D. *Ocimum sanctum* In: *Indian Medicinal Plants* 2nd ed. Pub. Lalit Mohan Basu. M.B. 49, Leader Road, Allahabad, India, **1935**, *3*:1965.

Kolte, A.Y., Sadekar, R.D., Barmase, B.S., Desai, V.F. and Kolte, B.R. Immunomo-dulating effect of dry powder of *Ocimum sanctum* and leaf gall of *Ficus racemosa* leaves in broilers naturally infected with IBD virus. *Ind. Vet. J.,* **1999**, *76*:84-86.

Krishnamurthy, T.R. Some pharmacological actions of an extract of *Ocimum sanctum. Ind. J. Phy. Pharm.,* **1959**, *3*:92-100.

Kumar, P., Singh, S.P., Doval, D.C., Singh, N. and Kohli, R.P. A clinical assessment of changes in cell-mediated immune response induced by Geriforte. *The Antiseptic,* **1982**, *10*:560.

Lahariya, A.K. and Rao, J.T. *In vitro* antimicrobial studies of the essential oils of *Cyperus scariosus* and *Ocimum basilicum.* . *Ind. Drugs,* **1979**,*16(7)*:150-152.

Lal, R.N., Sen, T.K. and Nigam, M.C. Gas chromatography of the essential oil of *Ocimum sanctum. Perfum Kosmet.,* **1978**, *59*:230.

Lasker, S. Clinical trial of an indigenous preparation in osteoarthrosis of knee. *Med. Surg.* **1981**, *8*:21.

Laurence, B.M., Hogg, J.W., Terhune, S.J. and Pichitakul, N. Essential oils and their constituents. The oils of *Ocimum sanctum* and *Ocimum basilicum* from Thailand. *Flavour Ind.,* **1972**, *3(l)*:47-49.

Laurence, D.R., Bennett, P.N. and Brown, M.J. Salicylic acids. In: *Inflammation, Arthritis and NSAIDs. Clinical Pharmacology.* 8th ed. Churchill Livingstone. Longman Singapore Publishers (Pte.) Ltd. Singapore, **1997**, pp. 255-257.

Lazarev, N.V. *Pharmacological Toxicology.* Quoted by Brekhman, I.I. and Dordymov, I.V. (see), **1958**, *21*:81.

Lemberkovics, E., Kery, A., Marczal, G., Simandi, B. and Szoke, E. Phytochemical evaluation of essential oils, medicinal plants and their preparations. *Acta. Pharm. Hung.,* **1998**, *68(3)*:141-149.

Leutenberer C and Leutenberger R. Abnormalities of mitosis, DNA metabolism and growth in human lung culture exposed to smoke from Marijuana cigarettes and their similarity with alterations evoked by tobacco cigarette smoke. Scientific Research on Cannabis. United Nationa Secretariat Publications. **1972**, No. 37:1-6.

Lim-Sylianco, C.Y., Panizares, I. and Jacano, A.P. Clastogenic effects of bone marrow erythrocytes of some medicinal plants. *Phillip. J. Sci.,* **1985**, *114(1-2)*:39-52.

Maheshwari, M.L., Singh, B.M., Gupta, R. and Chien, M. Essential oil of sacred basil (*Ocimum sanctum*). *Indian Perfumer.,* **1987**, *31*:137-145.

Malviya, B.K. and Gupta, P.L. Growth promoting properties of *Ocimum sanctum* Linn. *Ind. J. Pharmacol.,* **1971**, *33(6)*:126.

Mandal, S., Das, D.N., De, K., Ray, K, Roy, G., Chaudhuri, S.B., Sahana, C.C. and Chowdhuri, M.K. *Ocimum sanctum* Linn—a study on gastric ulceration and gastric secretion in rats. *Ind. J. Physiol. Pharmacol.,* **1993**, *37(1)*:91-92.

Mediratta, P.K. and Sharma, K.K. Effect of essential oil of the leaves and fixed oil of the seeds of *Ocimum sanctum* on immune responses. *J. Med. Aro. Plant Sci.,* **2000**, *22*:694-700.

Mediratta, P.K., Dewan, V., Bhattacharya, S.K., Gupta, V.S., Maiti, P.C. and Sen, P. Effect of *Ocimum sanctum* linn. on humoral immune response. *Ind. J. Med. Res.,* **1987**, *87*:384.

Mediratta, P.K., Sharma, K.K. and Singh, S. Evaluation of immunomodulatory potential of Ocimum sanctum seed oil and its possible mechanism of action. J. Ethnopharmacol. **2002**, *80*:15-20.

Mehta, A., Chopra, S., Mehta, P. and Kharaya, M.D. Antimicrobial activity of some essential oil against certain pathogenic bacteria. *Bull. Bot. Soc. Univ. Saugar,* **1978-79**, *14*:25-26.

Misra, N., Srivastava, A.K., Dixit, K.S., Singh, N. and Gupta, G.P. Plant drugs and biochemical changes during stress reaction. *Physiology of Human Performance. Proc. Nat. Symp. Physiol. Hum. Perfor.* (Sawhney, R.C., Sridharan, K. and Selvamurthy, W. eds) Publisher: Defence Institute of Physiology and Allied Sciences, Defence Research and Development Organization (DRDO), Govt. of India, Delhi, **1987**, pp. 104-108.

Misra. A., Misra. P.C. and Singh. N. Evaluation of "ayurvedic herbal drugs on the damage caused by free radicals". PhD Thesis, Department of Pharmacology and Therapeutics, K.G.M.C., Lucknow University, Lucknow, UP, India, **1998**.

Nadkarni, G.B. and Patwardhan, V.A. Fatty oil from the seeds of *Ocimum sanctum, Linn. Curr. Sci.,* **1952**, *21(3)*:68.

Nadkarni, K.M. *Ocimum sanctum* In: *Dr. K.M. Nadkarni's Indian Meteria Medica.* (1908) Revised and Enlarged by Nadkarni, A.K. Popular Prakashan Pvt. Ltd. 35C, Tardeo Road, Popular press Bulg., Bombay, **1982**, *1*:865-867.

Nand, S.K. Rastantra Sar. Tulsi. In: *Siddha Prajog Sangrah.* Gopal Ayurved Bhawan. Ajmer, Rajasthan, India, **1973**, *I*:162.

Narasimha Rao, B.G.V. and Nigam, S.S. *In vitro* antimicrobial efficiency of essential oils. *Ind. J. Med. Res.,* **1970**, *58(5)*:627-633.

Narasimha Rao, B.G.V. and Subba Rao, P. Efficacy of some essential oils on pathogenic fungi. *Flavour Ind.,* **1972**, *3(7)*:368-370.

Newmark, T.M. and Schulick, P. *Beyond Aspirin.* Hohm Press. Prescott, Arizona. **2000.**

Nigam, M.C., Handa, K.L. and Rao, P.R. Gas chromatography of the essential oil of seed basil. A Potential Source of Linalool in India. *Perfum Kosmet.,* **1970**, *51*:151-153.

Nwosu, M.O. and Okafor, J.l. Preliminary studies of the antifungal activities of some medicinal plants against *Basidiobolus* and some other pathogenic fungi. *Mycoses,* **1995**, *38(5-6)*:191-5

Offiah, V.N. and Chikwendu, U.A. Antidiarrhoeal effect of *Ocimum gratissimum* leaf extract in experimental animals. *J. Ethnopharmacol.,* **1999**, pp. 327-330.

Omoregbe, R.E., Ikuebe, O.M. and Ihimire, I.G. Antimicrobial activity of some medicinal plants extracts on *Escherichia coli, Salmonella paratyphi* and *Shigella dysenteriae. Afr. J. Med. Med. Sci,* **1996**, *25(4)*:373-375.

Ornish, D. Basil, Salads and Starters In: *Dr. Dean Ornish's Program For Reversing Heart Disease.* Ivy Books, Published by Ballantine Books, New York, **1996**, pp. 389-390.

Palit, G., Singh, S.P., Singh, N., Kohli, R.P. and Bhargava, K.P. Antiasthmatic potentials of *Ocimum sanctum* and *Terminalia belerica. Proc. XIVth Convention Indian Coll. Aller. Immunol.,* **1980**, pp. 10.

Palit, G., Singh, S.P., Singh, N., Kohli, R.P. and Bhargava, K.P. An experimental evaluation of antiasthmatic plant drugs from the ancient ayurvedic medicine. *Asp. Aller. Appl. Immunol.,* **1983**, *16*:36-41.

Panda, S. and Kar, A. *Ocimum sanctum* leaf extract in the regulation of thyroid function in the male mouse. *Pharmacol. Res.* **1998**, *38(2)*:107-110.

Papov, I.M. Clinical use of ginseng extract as adjuvant in revitalization therapies. *Proc. Int. Ginseng Symp.* The Central Research Institute, Republic of Korea, **1975**, pp. 115.

Patel, V.K. and Bhatt, H.V.K. Folklore therapeutic indigenous plants in periodontal disorders in India (review, experimental and clinical approach). *Int. J. Clin. Pharmacol. Ther. Toxicol.,* **1988**, *26(4)*:176-184.

Petkov, V. Possibilities for optimizing reactivity by pharmacological agents. *Symp. Gerontology, Lugano,* **1975**.

Prashar, R., Kumar, A., Banerjee, S. and Rao, A.R. Chemopreventive action by an extract from *Ocimum sanctum* on mouse skin papillomagenesis and its enhancement of skin glutathione S-transferase activity and acid soluble sulfydryl level. *Anticancer Drugs,* **1994**, *5(5)*:567-572.

Pushpangadan, P. and Sobti, S.N. Medicinal properties of *Ocimum* (Tulsi) species and some recent investigation of their efficacy. *Ind. Drugs,* **1977**, *14(11)*:207.

Rai, Y. Holy Basil Tulsi (A Herb) Printer, H.R. Gala at Navneet Press Ltd. Ahamadabad, Pub. S.R. Gala, for Navneet Publications (I) Ltd. Ahamadabad. **1988**, 126, 129.

Rajalakshmi, G., Sivanandam and Velachamy, G. Role of Tulsi (*Ocimum sanctum* Linn.) In: Management of Manjal Kamalai (Viral Hepatitis). *J. Res. Ayur. Sid.,* **1988**, *9*:118.

Ramasarma, T. Environmental stress and biochemical adaptation. *Biochem. Reviews,* **1978**, *49*:13-23.

Ramaswami, A.S. and Sirsi, M. Antitubercular activity of some natural products. *Ind. J. Pharm.,* **1967**, *29(5)*:157-159.

Rastogi, R.P. and Mehrotra, B.N. *Ocimum sanctum* In: *Compendium of Indian Medicinal Plants.* Publication and Information Directorate, CSIR, New Delhi, **1995a**, *4*:510.

Rastogi, R.P. and Mehrotra, B.N. *Ocimum sanctum* In: *Compendium of Indian Medicinal Plants.* Publication and Information Directorate, CSIR, New Delhi, **1995b**, *3*:455.

Reiter, M. and Brandt, W. Relaxant effects on tracheal and ileal smooth muscles of the guinea pig. *Arzneimittelforschung,* **1985**, *35(1A)*:408-14.

Robbins, J. Losing a war we could prevent. In: *Diet For A New America.* Stillpoint Publishing, Meetinghouse Road Walpole, N H, **1987**, pp. 248.

Robbins, S.R., Angell, M. and Kumar, V. Disease at the Cellular Level: Free Radical Mediation of Cell Injury. In: *Basic Pathology.* 3rd edn. Press of W.S. Saunders Company Philadelphia. Printed in Japan. Igaku-Shoin/Saunders International Edition. **1982**, pp. 9-13.

Roy, A.N., Sinha, B.P. and Gupta, K.C. The Inhibitory effect of plant juices on the infectivity of top necrosis virus of pea. *Ind. J. Microbiol.,* **1979,** *19*:198.

Roy, R.G., Madesayaa, N.M., Ghosh, R.B., Gopalakrishnan, D.V., Murty, N.M., Doraraj, T.J. and Sitaraman, N.L. Study on inhalation therapy by an indigenous compound on *P. vivax* and *P. falciparum* infections: A Preliminary Communication. *Ind. J. Med. Res.,* **1976,** *64(10)*:1451-1455.

Sakina, M.R., Dandiya, P.C., Hamdard, M.E. and Hameed A. Preliminary psychopharmacological evaluation of *Ocimum sanctum* leaf extract. *J. Ethnopharmacol.,* **1990,** *28(2)*:143-150.

Saksena, A.K., Nath, C. and Singh, N. Effect of *Ocimum sanctum* (Tulsi) on physical endurance during thermal stress. *Physiology of Human Performance. Proc. Nat. Symp. Physiol. Hum. Perfor.* (Sawhney, R.C., Sridharan, K. and Selvamurthy, W. eds) Publisher: Defence Institute of Physiology and Allied Sciences, Defence Research and Development Organization (DRDO), Govt. of India, Delhi, **1987,** pp. 109-113.

Samudralwar, D.L. and Garg, A.N. Minor and trace elemental determination in the Indian herbal and other medicinal preparations. *Biol. Trace Elem. Res.,* **1996,** *54(2)*:113-121.

Sankaran, J.R. Tefroli in the managment of viral hepatitis. *The Antiseptic,* **1980,** *77*:643.

Sarkar, A., Lavania, S.C., Pandey, D.N. and Pant, M.C. Changes in the blood lipid profile after administration of *Ocimum sanctum* (Tulsi) leaves in the normal albino rabbits. *Ind. J. Physiol. Pharmacol.,* **1994,** *38(4)*:311-312.

Sawhney, S.S., Suri, R.K. and Thind, T.S. Antimicrobial efficacy of some essential oils *In vitro. Ind. Drugs,* **1977,** *15(2)*:30-32.

Seethalakshmi, B., Narasappa, A.P. and Kenchaveerappa, S. Protective effect of *Ocimum sanctum* in experimental liver injury in albino rats. *Ind. J. Pharmacol.,* **1982,** *14(I)*:63.

Selye H. Stress: The physiology and pathology of exposure to stress. In: *A treatise based on the concept of general adaptation syndrome and diseases of adaptation. Acta-Inc.* Medical Publisher, Montreal, Canada, **1950,** pp. 316.

Selye, H. *The Psychosocial Environment and Psychosomatic Diseases.* L. Levi, Oxford University Press, London, New York, Toronto, **1971,** pp. 299.

Sembulingam, K., Sembulingam, P. and Namasivayam, A. Effect of *Ocimum sanctum* Linn. on noise induced changes in plasma corticosterone level. *Ind. J. Physiol. Pharmacol.,* **1997,** *41(2)*:139-143.

Sen, P., Maiti, P.C., Puri, S., Ray, A., Audulov, N.A. and Valdman, A.V. Mechanism of anti-stress activity of *Ocimum sanctum* Linn, eugenol and *Tinospora malabarica* in experimental animals. *Ind. J. Exp. Biol.,* **1992,** *30(7)*:592-596.

Seth, S., Johri, N., and Sundarmaram, K.R. . *Ind. J. Exp. Biol.,* **1981,** *319*:1975

Sharma, P.V. *Ocimum sanctum* In: *Dravyaguna Vijana (Vegetable Drugs).* Chaukhambha Bharti Academy, Chaukhambha Vishwabharti. Varanasi, **1999,** *2*:513-516, 709-711.

Sharma, S.K. and Wattal, B.L. Efficacy of some mucilaginous seeds as biological control agents against mosquito larvae. *J. Entomol. Res.,* **1979,** *3(2)*:172-176.

Shastri, M.N.D. Tulsi. In: *Garudapuranam* (English version). CS Series, Varanasi Vidyavilas Press, Varanasi, India, **1968,** pp. 672-673.

Shenoy, D.H. Role of Tulsi in the prevention of postoperative peritoneal adhesions. *Aryaavaidyan,* **1998,** *11*:218-222.

Siegel, R.K. Ginseng Abuse Syndrome. *J. Am. Med. Ass.,* **1979,** *241*:1614-1619.

Singh, A.B. Inhibitory activity of some plant extracts on the infectivity of papaya leaf reduction virus. *Acta. Phytopath. Hung. Ind. Sci.,* **1972,** *7*:175.

Singh, A.K., Dikshit, A., Sharma, M.L. and Dixit, S.N. Fungitoxic activity of some essential oils. *Econ. Bot.*, **1980**, *34(2)*:186-190.

Singh, K.V. and Pathak, R.K. Antimicrobial activity of some plant extracts. *Ind. Drugs Pharm.*, **1979**, *14(4)*:25.

Singh, N. Ayurveda - The Medicine of the Future (part II). *Probe*, **1986c**, *25(4)*:309-313.

Singh, N. Ayurveda - The medicine of the future (Part III). *Probe*, **1986a**, *26(4)*:241-243.

Singh, N. A comparative evaluation of the effect of some species of *Ocimum sanctum* on anoxia tolerance in albino rats. *36th Ann. Cong. Med. Plant Res., Gesellschaft Fuer Arzeneipflanzenforschung, Freiburg*, **1988**, pp. 28.

Singh, N., Agarwal, A.K., Lata, A. and Kohli, R.P. Evaluation of 'adaptogenic' properties of *Withania somnifera*. *Proc. Ind. Pharmacol. Soc.* **1976**, pp17.

Singh, N. A new concept on the possible therapy of stress disease with 'adaptogens´ (Anti-stress Drugs) of indigenous plant origin. *Curr. Med. Prac.*, **1981**, *25*:50-55.

Singh, N. A pharmaco-clinical evaluation of some Ayurvedic crude plant drugs as anti-stress agents and their usefulness in some stress diseases of man. *Ann. Nat. Acad. Ind. Med.*, **1986b**, *2(1)*:14-26.

Singh, N. and Abbas, S.S. Anti-fatigue effect of *Ocimum sanctum* in aging patients of arterial hypertension, rheumatoid arthritis, osteoarthritis. (Unpublished data). International Institute of Herbal Medicines, Lucknow, U.P. India, **1995a**.

Singh, N. and Abbas, S.S. Effect of *Ocimum sanctum* (Tulsi) in sex-related chronic fatigue syndrome (SRCFS) in young Indians. *J. Bio. Chem. Sci.*, **1995b**, *14*:184-187.

Singh, N. and Misra, N. Experimental Methods – Tools for assessment of anti-stress activity in medicinal plants. *J. Bio Chem. Res.*, **1993**, *12(182)*:124-127.

Singh, N. and Misra, N. Stress, stress-diseases and their possible remedy by anti-stress drugs (Adaptogens / Staminator) of plant origin. *Physiology of Human Performance. Proc. Nat. Symp. Physiol. Hum. Perfor.* (Sawhney, R.C., Sridharan, K. and Selvamurthy, W. eds) Publisher: Defence Institute of Physiology and Allied Sciences, Defence Research and Development Organization (DRDO), Govt. of India, Delhi, **1987**, pp. 89-94.

Singh, N. Anti-stress plants as anti-rheumatic agents. *8th SEPAL Cong. Rheumatol.* Bangkok, Thailand, **1984**, pp. 16.

Singh, N. Stress diseases and Herbal Medicines. *Proc. Conf. Curr. Biotech. Trends Med. Plants Res.*, **1993**, pp. 3.

Singh, N. *Withania somnifera* (Ashwagandha) – a rejuvenating herbal drug which enhances survival during stress – an adaptogen. *Int. J. Crude Drug Res.*, **1982**, *20*:29-35.

Singh, N., Gupta, M.L., Das, M. and Kohli, R.P. Preventive effect of some indigenous drugs on stress and aspirin induced gastric ulcers in albino rats. *Proc. Decennial Conf. Ind. Pharmacol. Soc.*, Calcutta. **1977a**, Abstract No. 171.

Singh, N., Kumar. P., Ahmad, S., Singh, R.P., Kohli, R.P. and Bhargava, K.P. Anti-stress plant drugs - A new approach in the treatment of stress disease. *Planta Medica*, **1982**, *45*:138.

Singh, N., Misra, N., Srivastava, A.K., Dixit, K.S. and Gupta, G.P. Effects of anti-stress plants on biochemical changes during stress reaction. *Ind. J. Pharmacol.*, **1991a**, *23(3)*:137-142.

Singh, N., Nath, R. and Kohli, R.P. Experimental evaluation of adaptogenic properties of *Ocimum sanctum*. *Proc. Decennial Conf. Ind. Pharmacol. Soc.*, Calcutta. **1977b**, Abstract No. 127.

Singh, N., Nath, R., Misra, N. and Kohli, R.P. An experimental evaluation of anti-stress effects of Geriforte. *Quart. J. Crude Drug Res.*, **1978**, *3*:125

Singh, N., Verma, P., Misra, N. and Nath, R. A comparative evaluation of some anti-stress agents of plant origin. Paper awarded "Dr. B. Mukerjee Award" for Best Paper on "Indigenous System of Medicine". *Ind. J. Pharmacol.*, **1991b**, *23*:99-103.

Singh, N., Vrat, S., Ali, B. and Bhargava, K.P. An assessment of biological effects of chronic use of cannabis (Marihuana) in human subjects. *Quart. J. Crude Drug Res.*, **1981**, *19(2-3)*:81-91.

Singh, P.P., Sharma, N.M. and Suri, B.K. Value of green leaves as source of available calcium. *Ind. J. Med. Res.*, **1969**, *57*:204-209.

Singh, R.B., Niaz, M.A., Rastogi, V., Singh, N. Postiglione, A. and Rastogi, S.S. Hypolipidemic and Antioxidant effects of fenugreek seeds and triphala as adjuncts to dietary therapy in patients with mild to moderate hypercholesterolemia. *Perfusion*, **1998**, *11*:124-130.

Singh, R.S. Tulsi. In: *"Vanaushadhi Nidarshika"* *(Ayurvedic Pharmacopeia)*. Publisher: HSS Vibhag UP. Bhargar Bhushan Press, Varanasi, India, **1983**, pp. 174.

Singh, S. and Majumdar, D.K. Evaluation of gastric antiulcer activity of fixed oil of *Ocimum sanctum* (holy basil). *J. Ethnopharmacol.*, **1999**, *65*:13-19.

Singh, S. and Majumdar, D.K. Evaluation of anti-inflammatory activity of fatty acids of *Ocimum sanctum* fixed oil. *Ind. J. Exp. Biol.*, **1997**, *35(4)*:380-383.

Singh, S. Comparative evaluation of anti-inflammatory potential of fixed oil of different species of *Ocimum* and its possible mechanism of action. *Ind. J. Exp. Biol.*, **1998**, *36(10)*:1028-1031.

Singh, S., Majumdar, D.K. and Yadav, M.R. Chemical and pharmacological studies on fixed oil of *Ocimum sanctum*. *Ind. J. Exp. Biol.*, **1996**, *34(12)*:1212-1215.

Singh, S.P. and Singh, N. Experimental evaluation of adaptogenic properties of *Ocimum sanctum*. *Ind. J. Pharmacol.*, **1978**, *10*:74.

Singh, S.P., Sinha, K.N., Singh, N. and Kohli, R.P. *Inula racemosa* (Pushkarmool), *Terminalia belerica* (Vibhitaki) and *Ocimum sanctum* (Tulsi) — A preliminary clinical trial in asthma patients. *Proc. Int. Sem. Clin. Pharmacol. Dev. Count. K.G.M.C., Lucknow, India.* (Saxena, R.C., Gupta, T.K. and Dixit, K.S. eds), **1986**, *I*:18-21.

Singh, T.J., Gupta, P.D., Khan, S.Y. and Misra, K.C. Preliminary pharmacological investigation of *Ocimum sanctum. Ind. J. Pharm.*, **1970**, *32(4)*:93.

Singh, V., Singh, A., Nath, R., Misra, N., Dixit, K.S. and Singh, N. Effect of some anti-stress plant drugs on intestinal transit. *J. Biol. Chem Res.*, **1991c**, *10(4)*:601-602.

Sirtori, A.S., Rush, M.N. and Sudev, S.T. The Saponins of the seed of four lupin species. *J. Plant Foods*, **1979**, *3*:181-190.

Siurin, S.A. Effects of essential oil on lipid peroxidation and lipid metabolism in patients with chronic bronchitis. *Klin. Med. (Mosk)*, **1997**, *75(10)*:43-45.

Sivarajan, V.V. and Balachandran, I. Tulsi. In: *Ayurvedic Drugs and their Plant Sources*. Oxford FBH Publishing Co. Pvt. Ltd., New Delhi, India, **1994**, pp. 485-486.

Srivastava, A.K., Chandra, M., Pandiya, S.N., Dixit, K.S., Singh, N., Husain, A. and Bhargava, K.P. A Preliminary clinical trial of *Ocimum sanctum* (Tulsi) extract in stress related hypertensive patients. P*Proc. Int. Sem. Clin. Pharmacol. Dev. Count. K.G.M.C, Lucknow, India.* (Saxena, R.C., Gupta, T.K. and Dixit, K.S. eds), **1986**, *II*:36-38.

Srivastava, A.K., Singh, N. and Bhargava, K.P. "Pharmacology of Stress" Doctor of Medicine (Thesis MD), Lucknow University, India, **1984**.

Srivastava, H.N. *Ocimum sanctum*. In: *Practical Botany II*. Pradeep Jain for Pradeep Publications, Jalandhar, Print. Rajkamat Jain, Apex Printing Press, Jalandhar, India, **1988**, pp. 210-211.

Steinberg, D. Antioxidant vitamins and coronary heart disease. *N. Eng. J. Med.*, **1993**, *328*:1487-1489.

Suri, R.K. and Thind, T.S. *In vitro* antifungal efficacy of four essential oils. *Ind. Perfum.*, **1979a**, *23(2)*:138-140.

Suri, R.K. and Thind, T.S. Antibacterial activity of some essential oils. *Ind. Drugs Pharm. Ind.*, **1978**, *13(6)*:25-28.

Suri, R.K. and Thind. T.S. *In vitro* antifungal efficacy of some essential oils. *East. Pharm.*, **1979b**, *22(257)*:109-110.

Susrut, Sutrasthana. In: *Sushruta Samhita*. Nimayasagar Press, Bombay, **1938**, *Sutra 46/ 234*.

Tierney, L., Mc Phee, S.J. and Papadakis, M. Interstitial nephritis, thrombocytopenia. In: *Curr. Med. Diag. Treat*. Appleton & Lange, **1995**, *34*:780, 464.

Tripathi, R.K.R. and Tripathi, R.N. Reduction in bean common mosaic virus (BCMV) infectivity vis-a-vis crude leaf extract of some higher plants. *Experientia*, **1982**, *38*:349.

Tulsi Kavacham Quoted by Dymock, W. Tulsi In: *Pharmacograhica Indica. A History of Principal Drugs of Vegetable Origin*. Kogan Paul Trench. Trubner and Co., Ltd., London, **1892**, *3*:86.

Uma Devi, P., Ganasoundari, A., Rao, B.S. and Srinivasan, K.K. In vivo radioprotection by *Ocimum* flavonoids: survival of mice. *Radiat. Res.*, **1999**, *151(1)*:74-78.

Vaidya, B.G. Tulsiyadiverga. Uttarrardha. In: *Nighantu Adarsha*. CB Academy, Gopal Mandir Lane, Printer: Vidyavilas Press. Varanasi, **1985**, pp. 265-287.

Varier, P.S. *Ocimum sanctum* In: *Indian Medicinal Plants*. (Warrier, P.K., Nambiar, V.P.K. and Ramankutty, C. Arya Vaidya Sala Kottakkal eds.), Printed in India at Krystal Offset, Chennai. Pub. Orient Longman Limited 160 Anna Salai, Chennai, **1996**, *4*:168-171.

Vedavyasa, Maharshi. Tulsi. In: *Garudapuranam*. CS Series, Varanasi, Vidyavilas Press, **1964**, pp. 332-334.

Vedavyasa, Maharshi. Tulsi. In: *Vishhramantraudham Agnipuranam*. Publisher: CS Series, Vidyavilas Press. Varanasi, **1966**, pp. 442.

Vedvyasa B. Tulsi. In: *Padmapuranam*. GB Geetapress, Gorakhpur, India, **1960**.

Vohara, S.B., Garg, S.K. and Chaudhury, R.R. Antifertility screening of plants. Part III. Effect of six indigenous plants on early pregnancy in albino rats. *Ind. J. Med. Res.,* **1969**, *57*:893-899.

Vohara, S.B., Garg, S.K. and Chaudhury, R.R. Effect of six indigenous plants on early pregnancy in albino rats. *Ind. J. Pharm.,* **1968**, *30*:287.

World Health Organization. Preamble to the Constitution of the World Health Organization as adopted by International Health Conference, New York, 19-22 June, **1946**; (*Official Records of the WHO*, no. 2, pp. 100).

World Health Organization. The promotion and development of traditional medicine. Technical Report Series no. 622, WHO Geneva, **1978**.

Yamasaki, K., Nakano, M., Kawahata, T., Mori, H., Otake, T., Ueba, N,, Oishi, I., Inami, R., Yamane, M., Nakamura, M., Murata, H. and Nakanishi, T. Anti-HIV-1 activity of herbs in Labiatae. *Biol. Pharm. Bull.,* **1998**, *21(8)*:829-833.

Index